BIALYSTOK TO BIRKENAU

Central Europe, borders of 1937.

BIALYSTOK
TO
BIRKENAU

The Holocaust Journey of Michel Mielnicki

as told to
JOHN MUNRO

Introduction by
SIR MARTIN GILBERT

RONSDALE PRESS & VANCOUVER HOLOCAUST EDUCATION CENTRE

BIALYSTOK TO BIRKENAU
© 2000 Michel Mielnicki and John Munro

RONSDALE PRESS
3350 West 21st Avenue
Vancouver, B.C. Canada
V6S 1G7

Set in Garamond: 12pt on 14.5
Typesetting and Cover Design: Metaform, Vancouver, B.C.
Printing: Hignell Printing, Winnipeg, Manitoba

Ronsdale Press wishes to thank the Canada Council for the Arts, the Government of Canada through the Book Publishing Industry Development Program (BPIDP), and the Province of British Columbia through the British Columbia Arts Council for their support of its publishing program.

CANADIAN CATALOGUING IN PUBLICATION DATA
Mielnicki, Michel, 1927 -
    Bialystok to Birkenau

Includes index.
ISBN 0-921870-77-9

1. Mielnicki, Michel, 1927- 2. Holocaust, Jewish (1939-1945) – Personal narratives.
3. Holocaust survivors – Canada – Biography. I. Munro, John A., 1938-
II. Title.
D804.196.M55 2000   940.52'18'092   C00-910585-9

To the beloved memories
of my father Chaim, my mother Esther, my brother Aleksei,
and our former friends and neighbours in our hometown
of Wasilkow, Poland, all but three of whom
were murdered by fascist Poles and German Nazis
in World War II.

TABLE OF CONTENTS

INTRODUCTION

BY SIR MARTIN GILBERT C.B.E., D.LITT

It is a great honour to be asked to write this introduction. When I met Michel Mielnicki in Vancouver, I could feel the strength of his character, and something of the pain of his suffering. Since 1945 he has been a Holocaust witness, which, as he recounts, "has been its own kind of hell."

Michel was born in a small town, Wasilkow, in eastern Poland, a few miles from the city of Bialystok. Of the town's 5,000 inhabitants, 1,500 were Jews. After the German conquest of that region in the summer of 1941, he spent fourteen months in the ghetto of Pruzany. From there he was deported with his family to Auschwitz, where his father was murdered. Later he was a slave labourer, first at Buna, then at Mittelbau-Dora. He was liberated in Belsen.

Even from this brief outline of Michel's story it is clear that he has much to tell. The details in the book are rich and rewarding. He describes his childhood in Wasilkow with particular charm — the lost world of pre-War Polish Jewry. Even during the War, his memories of the earlier years were to haunt, and to serve him: "Sauerkraut, warmed in a little oil, then mixed with mashed potatoes, was something I fantasized about as a half-starved inmate in Birkenau, or as I lay at death's door too weak from hunger even to move from my bunk when the British army liberated Bergen-Belsen in 1945." It was memories of his mother's cooking, he attests, that gave him, while in Birkenau, "the saliva necessary to chew bread that was at least twenty-five percent sawdust."

Childhood, with recollections of dodging from time to time the Polish anti-Semites while on the way to school, was followed by the German invasion of Poland, when Michel was twelve. He vividly recalls how his father took him into Bialystok to see the bodies of some of the several hundred Jews who had been murdered there in the few days before the German army was replaced by the Soviet forces. "I don't know whether my father saw our future clearly then or not, but in his own very particular way, he was preparing me to survive it by making me, at least in part, immune to some of its horrors."

. The period of Soviet rule, from September 1939 to June 1941, saw Michel's father working for the Soviet secret service. "It is my firm belief that no one was ever murdered at my father's behest," Michel asserts. But so hated did his father become that "because I was Chaim Mielnicki's son, I found myself the target of Polish bullets when I returned to Bialystok after the War."

Soviet rule brought unexpected benefits. This part of Michel's memoirs, which includes his bar mitzvah, throws light on a neglected period of Jewish history. Among other things, the pre-War Polish quota system for Jews in higher education was swept away. He himself, aged fourteen, took up photography, and, by taking photographs of Russian soldiers that they would then send to their parents and sweethearts, earned enough money to buy a motorcycle.

The German occupation began in June 1941. With his blond hair masking his Jewishness, Michel joined a bread queue. A Polish Christian classmate volunteered to help the Nazi guard point out Jews in the lineup, and Michel was forced to leave it.

The torments of the Holocaust did not destroy Michel's sense of right and wrong. For me, the two most powerful sentences in his book are his statement: "When I was liberated from Bergen-Belsen in 1945, I could not bring myself to join my colleagues in capturing and killing our former *SS* guards. I turned away when they were being beaten to death, saying that this was a matter for God, or for the law courts."

It was the Poles, not Germans, who caused the first mass murder of Jews in Wasilkow. Michel does honour to those first victims by naming them (the naming of names is so important in the Jewish recognition of the merit and value of each individual). Thus he identifies "the orchestra leader, Avreml Polak, his brother-in-law, Dovid Shrabinski, the crate-maker's son, Motke Spektor, Archik the Greek, and a fine artist by the name of Shie Mongele," dragged from their beds and clubbed to death in the yard of a textile factory. "How do I know this? I saw their bodies." Not only that, as one of those who were forced to bury the bodies, Michel was present when the two German soldiers brutally assaulted and then burned to death the community's much-respected *shochet* (ritual slaughterman), Walper Kowalski. "I was haunted by the smell of burning flesh. Of course, I did not yet know that I was going to a crematorium where I would smell it all the time, day and night."

With Wasilkow under German rule, Michel witnessed yet another terrifying pogrom carried out by local Poles. He saw from his window "one of our very pregnant neighbours being beaten to death with clubs and two-by-fours," and heard a Pole call out to his fellow-looters as they rampaged through the house next door: "Don't damage, don't damage, it's all ours." By the time German soldiers intervened to stop this Polish slaughter of Jews, two dozen more had been murdered.

From Wasilkow, the Mielnickis went to Bialystok. Michel's descriptions of the Bialystok ghetto are haunting. He tells of the newborn babies "whose little lives had been snuffed out by mothers unable to feed them". From Bialystok, to avoid Chaim Mielnicki's arrest on Gestapo orders, the family went to Pruzany, another ghetto, and another stage of the harrowing saga. There, during the next fourteen months, hunger and privation took its steady, relentless toll. "By the time we left Pruzany in December 1942, we all looked like ragamuffins — which served further to destroy our self-esteem, and thus weaken by another degree or two our ability to resist the Nazi death machine."

In December 1942 came the order for transfer to "work" in Germany for 3,000 of the ghetto inmates. "We were optimistic about our futures. Even Mother, who was by this time emaciated, thought we might be better off in a labour camp." She told her family: "At least we'll have our daily bread, and soup, and things like that. They're not going to let us starve in a labour camp." But this "labour camp" destination was a cruel Nazi deception. Michel had never travelled by train before. His description of the agonies of the journey constitutes one of the more powerful pages in the book: his own torment and that of those around him. "I was so far out of it that I didn't even know that only an arm's length away my mother was dying."

At the selection at the railway ramp at Auschwitz, Michel's father was seized by the neck by a cane-wielding non-commissioned officer in charge of the selection that day, immaculately dressed *SS*-Sergeant Kuhnemann. "On the side, you dirty Jew," Kuhnemann screamed at Michel's father, "and began to smash him across the head." Chaim Mielnicki was forty-seven years old. "I have never recovered from his loss," Michel avers. "Nor have I ever been able to reconcile myself to the obscene and mocking death inflicted upon him by the forces of Hitlerian maleficence." Michel's mother also died that day, possibly on a stretcher on the ramp.

Michel, his brother Aleksei, and their sister Lenka, were selected for slave labour. Michel's description of Birkenau is true and horrific. "My God, I once saw a prisoner sent to the crematorium for having boils on his neck." He witnessed two fellow-prisoners pushed upside down through the toilet seat until their heads were under the excrement, and then held down with long poles "until the bubbles stopped coming through." Other prisoners were then ordered to take out the bodies, hose them down, and lay them out at roll call.

At the slave labour camp at Buna, a few miles from Auschwitz, a British prisoner of war said to Michel: "You're going to die, you

goddamned Jew." As I write these words, I can only hang my head
in shame at a fellow-Briton's ugliness. I might note, however, that
another prisoner of war at Buna, British Sergeant John Coward,
was given the Righteous Gentile award by the State of Israel for
saving Jews.

After Buna, which he describes with stark honesty — the
hallmark of his book — Michel survived a death march, and also
the Mittelbau-Dora slave labour camp, at which he was one of
tens of thousands of slave labourers making Hitler's V1 and V2
"revenge weapons" (flying bombs and rockets). It was a camp in
which more slave labourers died — 20,000 in all — than Britons
and Belgians blown up when the weapons landed.

Michel's war ended in Belsen. He has serious criticisms of the
efforts of his British liberators in saving lives, though the efforts of
the British doctors and nurses have been praised by others.
Michel's conclusion with regard to the British effort is unequivo-
cal: "We deserved better". And he was there.

After escaping from a death march, Michel's sister Lenka had
been saved in hiding by a Sudeten-German woman for more than
four months, until liberation. The woman's son was a German
army officer. Michel and Lenka were reunited because both had
written to an uncle in New Jersey to say that they were alive. The
uncle had been able to put them in touch with each other. Such
were the small miracles of those years.

Michel travelled to Bialystok. He was advised not to go on to
his home town, Wasilkow. A newly wed Jewish couple who had
done so, hoping to regain their family home, had been murdered
— beheaded by local Poles. But return he did, and had the amazing good fortune of being given $500 (a considerable sum in those
days) for his two family properties: a second small miracle. More
than a thousand Jews had been murdered after they had gone back
to their home towns in Poland in 1945. Michel himself was shot
at, one night, in Bialystok. Both bullets missed. Then, on the train
westward, a Polish thug pointed a machine gun at him. "Are you

a Jew?" he demanded. Michel sneered in reply: "What? Are you trying to insult me?" and was left alone. That incident decided him to leave Poland for ever. He went to France with his sister. In Paris he met his future wife, June, herself a survivor, originally from Cracow. In 1953 they emigrated to Canada. Lenka stayed in France, and later emigrated to Israel.

In 1989, the notorious SS-Sergeant Kuhnemann, from Birkenau, was recognized by another Auschwitz inmate, Rudy Vrba, singing on stage during the performance of an opera in Duisburg, Germany. Michel went to Germany to give evidence against him. Ironically, both Vrba and Michel were then (and now) living in Vancouver. Michel comments: "Kuhnemann is now in his late seventies, or early eighties, too old, under German law, to be sent to jail. This SS-criminal will die at home, surrounded by his loving family. I don't want revenge, but I would like a little justice after all these years."

Kuhnemann's trial had one extraordinary sequel. Michel mentioned his brother Aleksei to the German prosecutor. Visiting Auschwitz some months later, the prosecutor found that Aleksei had been there earlier to register for compensation. He was alive, a Soviet citizen living in Ivano-Frankovsk (formerly the Polish city of Stanislawow). Michel had given up his brother for dead. In fact he had survived Mauthausen, been arrested after liberation by the Russians, near Warsaw, and been conscripted into the Soviet Army. In 1992 Michel visited Aleksei. They had not met for fifty years, since Birkenau.

In these pages, as one follows Michel from place to place, from Wasilkow to Bialystok, from Bialystok to Pruzany, from Pruzany to Birkenau, and then on to Buna, Mittelbau-Dora and Belsen, one is in the presence of great evil, and great courage. This is a story, not only of survival, but of the lives, qualities, enthusiasm and Jewish hearts that were destroyed in the twentieth century: the century which brought science, medicine and communications forward as never before, yet also saw the backward march of mankind. One can only pray that the twenty-first century will be spared such horrors. Reading this book will help show the generations now coming to adulthood just how necessary it is to be eternally vigilant.

MERTON COLLEGE
OXFORD
7 JANUARY 2000

PREFACE

This is a book that I have been promising to do for a very long time. Over the years, and especially since my wife June and I came, with our children Alain and Vivian, to live in Vancouver in 1966, people with whom I have shared fragments of my story of persecution by Polish anti-Semites and Nazi Germans during World War II invariably have said, "Michel, you have to write this down before it's too late. It's important. It's dynamite. Write it down and I'll buy your book." Well, as I was to discover, it's one thing to say that you are going to write a book, and quite another thing actually to do so, especially if the language in which you are trying to write is your sixth. Friends tried to help by tape-recording interviews with me, or by encouraging me to tape-record the talks I give to students as part of the program of the Vancouver Holocaust Education Centre. I had all these transcribed, but the mound of paper that resulted didn't make a book. Various professional writers approached me with offers of assistance or to buy the rights to my story, but, for reasons that I didn't entirely understand, I turned them down.

I think now that I simply wasn't ready to proceed until the right person came along. Certainly, when finally I was introduced to historian-writer John Munro in August 1995, I knew in my heart that the time had come to get on with the job. What I didn't know was the cost involved. I am not talking about money here, but emotion. Reliving the full detail of my experiences in the Holocaust has been profoundly depressing for me. In our months of interviews, John Munro probed my memory as I never thought possible, and I have shared with him, as with no other person, all the secrets of my life. It was John Munro who brought order to the chaos of my thoughts about the past, and together we have made the book that now is laid before you. I am further grateful that at last I have been able to complete a promise made more than half a century ago that I would bear full witness to the unspeakable horrors inflicted upon the Jewish people by the Hitlerian hordes.

Of course, I could have accomplished nothing at all without the love and encouragement of my wife June, with whom I have now enjoyed fifty years of wedded bliss. My wonderful children, Alain and Vivian, have been equally supportive of this project. Thanks too must go to my son-in-law, Dr. Jeffrey Claman, as well as to Dr. Robert Krell, Dr. Peter Gary, professors Doug Beardsley and William Nicholls, and historian Marvin Lyons, who read and commented on this manuscript. My editor assures me that their advice was helpful indeed. Special thanks must also go to my friend Phyllis Hamlett, who made a valiant effort to help me put my story down on paper before John Munro took this project in hand. There are many others, who, by word and deed, have encouraged me as well. I hope they all find satisfaction in the knowledge that royalties from the sale of this book will go to the establishment of a scholarship fund for the descendants of Holocaust survivors, in the names of myself and my wife, June Mielnicki, who is herself a survivor.

MICHEL MIELNICKI
VANCOUVER, BRITISH COLUMBIA
1 JANUARY 2000

CHAPTER I

MY FATHER'S SON

"On the side, you dirty Jew": words forever seared in my brain by *SS Unterscharführer* Heinrich Kuhnemann, as he tore my father from me with the crook of his cane in a "selection" of those to be immediately gassed and burned. When last I saw him — beside the dark and fetid freight car that had transported us into a surreal world of searchlights, high-voltage fences, snarling German wolfhounds, and their black-shirted masters — Chaim Mielnicki was but forty-seven years of age. And I have never recovered from his loss. Nor have I ever been able to reconcile myself to the obscene and mocking death inflicted upon him by the forces of Hitlerian maleficence. Such a vital, decent, intelligent, devoted, hardworking man, my father, who had always seemed to me, his youngest child, the very essence of *Chaim*, his given name — as in "*L'chaim*," the traditional Jewish toast "To life."

Now, more than a half-century later, in attempting to write about my own life and experiences as a Holocaust survivor, I have come to realize, as never before, that the Nazis not only murdered my father and desecrated his remains on that brutal night in December 1942, they stole our family's history in the process. The sad fact is that I know virtually nothing about my antecedents. Always busy — out early in the morning and coming home late at night — my father was not a man to sit and reminisce. He would take the time to answer my questions, but as a boy — I was just fifteen when I entered the gates of hell at Auschwitz/Birkenau — I never had the presence of mind to ask him about his parents, or grandparents, or even what it was like to grow up in Tsarist Russia. It well may be that our family name, Mielnicki, is derived from the Russian word for a miller — *melnik* — but I don't know if any of our ancestors were actually millers, or the circumstances that originally allowed our family to live in Rzhev (an historic Russian town, 180 or so kilometres from Moscow on the upper Volga River), well beyond the Pale of Settlement (the boundaries established in Russian law to limit Jewish settlement). I do know that Chaim Mielnicki was one of eight children (seven boys and one girl), and that he was born in 1895 — although I don't know the day or the month (so far as I remember, we never celebrated his birthday). I also know that in 1908, following the murder of my grandfather in a local pogrom, five of my father's brothers, his sister, and my grandmother, added their number to the flood of Russian Jews emigrating to America in search of lives that would be free from the indiscriminate killing of our people that followed the political upheavals, repression, and famine that came in the wake of Russia's humiliating defeats in the Russo-Japanese War of 1904-05.

Apparently, my father (the fifth son, who was thirteen years old at the time) was left behind to look after Shmulke (the second son) who, at seventeen or eighteen, was too ill to gain admission to the United States. Possibly he had tuberculosis, which was a common enough disease at the time — I don't know. In any event, in 1910 or thereabouts, Shmulke, obviously recovered or in remission, moved south to settle just outside Bialystok in Russia's Polish territories, where he married, bought a house, and fathered four children.

Trooper Chaim Mielnicki, 1st St. Petersburg Lancers, c.1915.

Chaim (my father) would have been fifteen years old in 1910. Possibly, once Shmulke was well enough to travel, it was intended that the two brothers use proceeds from the sale of family property in Rzhev's Jewish ghetto (if indeed there was any left) to join the others in upstate New York, where they finally settled — again I don't know. What I do know is that my father lied about his age to enlist in the imperial army of Tsar Nicholas II — a fate young Jewish males normally went to great lengths to avoid (sometimes deliberately crippling themselves when conscripted so that they would be rejected as medically unfit). However, with his brother now departed, and his family in the States possibly not yet able to help in any substantial way, it would appear that Chaim not only found himself alone, but in dire straits.

I remember him once saying: "To have food, clothes, and a bed to sleep in, you had to pay the price." Not that he, at least in retrospect, regretted the physical rigour, harsh discipline, long hours, and total regimentation that were a cavalryman's lot. He told me that these were valuable things for a young man to experience — but not as a career path! Given the man I came to know as my father, it would seem reasonable to assume as well that he volunteered for military service because he was attracted by the adventure of it all. This was still the age of "The Charge of the Light Brigade," not the atomic bomb. Whatever the case, when the First World War broke out in August 1914, my father was a trooper in the elite 1st St. Petersburg Lancer Regiment (Rzhev).

The above photograph shows Trooper Mielnicki, tall and strong, in his flamboyant, scarlet and blue hussar's dress uniform. The medal on the far right side of his tunic is for swordsmanship; that beside it, his certification as a sharpshooter. The larger one in the centre which carries the image of the Tsar, however, is the Nicholas II decoration for valour — apparently an unusual distinction for a Jew, however brave his deeds, given the virulently anti-Semitic command structure of the Russian army. But then, I think that Chaim Mielnicki was probably a most unusual young man to be in the 1st St. Petersburg Lancers in the first place.

I don't know for certain which battles he fought in, but from what little Father said to my brother or to me (when, with little boys' fascination for such things, we asked him about his bullet scars), they were all against the Austro-Hungarians. Indeed, it was his feat of courage in the wake of one of these bloody encounters that resulted in his medal for heroism. Although seriously injured himself, Trooper Mielnicki risked his life to save seventeen of his more severely disabled comrades by dragging each of them to safety with his one good arm when a flash flood hit the gully in which they were sheltering. Back in action a month or two later, he again found himself in the sights of an opposing sniper. Too badly wounded this time to escape, he was captured by Hungarian hussars. In that he was held as a prisoner of war in Austria for over two years, and that the war between Russia and the Central Powers effectively ended when the Bolsheviks negotiated an armistice with Germany in December 1917, I suspect this may have been at the Battle of Tarnopol in September 1915.

One thing, however, is certain: the wholesale slaughter of humanity on the Eastern Front left its mark on Chaim Mielnicki. It is estimated that Russia lost nearly two million dead and five million wounded in the conflict. (According to Sir Martin Gilbert in *The Dent Atlas of Jewish History*, 650,000 Jews served in the Russian army in World War I, of whom 100,000 were killed — many of them no doubt by the 340,000 Jews who fought in the Austro-Hungarian army, of whom 40,000 were killed.) What is more, two and a half million Russian soldiers wound up in primitive German and Austro-Hungarian prisoner of war camps, where they died by the tens of thousands from typhoid fever, influenza, and other contagious diseases. In prison camp, my father was a member of a detail assigned to collect and bury the bodies of his comrades. All that he had experienced in seven years of military service eventually turned Chaim into a pacifist, not in the sense that he wouldn't defend himself or his family if he were able to do so — running away from a fight was not his style — but that he no longer believed in war as a means of settling national or ideological disputes.

———

Fortunately for Father, in 1918, unlike the situation in 1945, there was no forced repatriation of Russian prisoners of war to the Soviet Union. Had there been, he would have found himself in the middle of a civil war — no doubt, if given the choice, on the Bolshevik side. As it was, when Chaim was released, he initially stayed in Vienna, which contained a large, historic, and flourishing Jewish community of about 175,000 people. What he did there I don't know, but he apparently made some money, and had a good time. He was only twenty-three, still very military in appearance, and very dashing. (Many people later told me that when my father came to Bialystok in the summer of 1918, he was one of the top dancers in the waltz.)

As to his choice of an area in which to settle, Bialystok was as close as he could come to returning to Russia without actually doing so. (The Bolsheviks had ceded Bialystok and its surrounding Polish provinces to the Germans under the terms of the Treaty of Brest-Litovsk on 3 March 1918.) Besides, it is distinctly possible that the 1st St. Petersburg Lancers were stationed or on manoeuvres in the Bialystok area before 1914. So he might have had some connections there, in addition to his brother Shmulke, who lived nearby, and at least one cousin, Pejsach Melnicki (different spelling, same family), who was a prominent Bialystoker, serving many years on the executive committee of the local *Kehilla* (the elected body that governed purely Jewish affairs) and as vice-chairman of the large and influential Bialystok Craftsmen's Association.

No doubt also important to his decision (or at least a factor in it) was the fact that in 1918 approximately half of Bialystok's

75,000-plus population were Jews. According to *The Encyclopedia Judaica*, "In 1921, 93% of the businessmen in Bialystok were Jewish, and 89% of the industrial plants [which were many, and mainly involved in textile manufacturing] were Jewish-owned." Finally, in that my father had yet to master the Polish language, there was an obvious advantage in the fact that the majority of Bialystokers, whether Jewish or gentile, were Russian-speaking — due to fifty years of official Russification prior to the First World War.

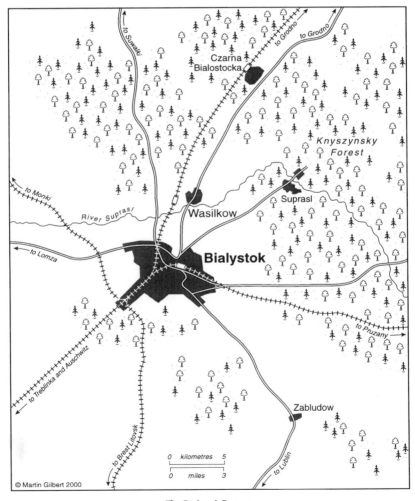

The Bialystok Region.

I do know that my father concluded soon after his arrival that the city proper was unsuitable for his immediate purposes, which involved the illegal manufacture and sale of vodka. The community that he chose instead was the sleepy little town of Wasilkow (population 5,000), seven kilometres northwest of Bialystok, on the main road from Warsaw to Vilna and St. Petersburg. Maybe the German military authority was less omnipresent there than in Bialystok proper — I don't know. I do know that Wasilkow was not particularly prosperous in 1918, and that unemployment was high. Possibly the town's location on a bend of the Suprasl River, which was wide and clean, and its proximity to nearby pine forests and lakes, were factors in the calculations of a bootlegger setting up a new business. Possibly also, the fact that Wasilkow was a popular, year-round, day-trip destination for Bialystokers who wanted to do a little swimming, fishing, rowing, hiking, or cross-country skiing (in the winter, this was big-snow country) created a steady demand for vodka. Again, I don't know.

It would seem logical, however, to assume that Chaim's choice of location was greatly influenced by the presence in Wasilkow of his brother Shmulke, who would have had an intimate knowledge of the lay of the land (i.e., the strength, attitudes, effectiveness, and corruptibility of the German military, the location of abandoned buildings suitable for a distilling operation, the availability and names of men to work in the plant, and of carters to move the product, etc.). Not that I was ever told any of the actual details of how my father's illicit trade worked in practice, but it seems reasonable to assume that in the two years before the administrative authority of the new Polish government became a reality, the combined thirsts of the metropolitan Bialystok population and of the retreating and competing armies in the region — German, White Russian, Soviet, Ukrainian, Polish — created a demand for vodka no combination of distillers could supply. (All of which ended when Bialystok finally and formally became part of a reconstituted independent Poland with the defeat of the Red

Army by the Polish armed forces under Marshal Jozef Pilsudski in October 1920.)

I have no doubt that there had to have been great risks, both physical and financial, in large-scale bootlegging. We've all seen movies or read books about the Prohibition period in the United States. Well, imagine all that in a *Dr. Zhivago* setting, and something approaching my father's situation might begin to emerge — apparently nothing that Chaim Mielnicki couldn't handle. Possibly, his reputation as a Russian war hero (which was still much talked about in Wasilkow when I was a boy) gave him a certain advantage when it came to dealing with the local military officials — to say nothing of resident thugs and bandits. It probably also didn't hurt that he always carried a large pistol in his belt, but he was, in any event, one tough guy. I remember the occasion in 1935, when he was attacked outside one of Wasilkow's taverns by a couple of drunken gentiles, who were looking to end their evening of merry-making by beating up a Jew. Any Jew. Chaim took a quick step back, grabbed each one by the hair, and smashed their heads together, leaving them lying in the road to consider, when they regained consciousness, the foolhardiness of their action. He was forty years old at the time.

Certainly, my father appears to have made a lot of money as the distiller of illegal spirits, and all of it tax-free. Unfortunately, with the final triumph of the Bolsheviks in the Russian Civil War in 1920, and the introduction of a new, stable currency, the *zloty*, in Poland in 1924, much of it became unusable. When I was a young boy, I used to while away the hours playing with stacks of large-denomination, but totally worthless Tsarist roubles. Nevertheless, there was enough of the real stuff left at the end of the day for my father to become a legitimate businessman.

I don't recall my father having any particular enemies in the local Christian community, at least before the Russian occupation in 1939. My father's gentile friends, both Polish and Russian, liked him because he was a man of action, full of energy and rough humour. They called him by his nickname, *Pitukh* (Rooster), from his days as a bugler in the St. Petersburg Lancers, which, among other things, involved sounding reveille each morning. It was a name that suited him — in his prime, Chaim Mielnicki was very much a cock of the walk who was more Russian than the Russians in everything that he did. There was hardly a man he couldn't out-fight, outdrink, outride, outswim, or out-who-knows-what-else.

I remember the time, when I was five or six years old, that a Polish peasant, a Christian (the peasants who lived in our area were all either Polish Roman Catholics or White Russian Orthodox), came to see my father in a state of great distress. He'd just been in a freak accident on the Bialystok Road (our main street), in which his horse had been so badly injured that the policeman on duty had to shoot it. (In fact, the horse had been disemboweled by a sharp piece of wood. I remember all this because, when my older brother took me out to look at it, its guts were lying all over the road.) For the farmer, the loss of his horse meant ruin. He couldn't plough or plant his fields without it.

My father listened patiently to his lament, gave him a glass of vodka, and told him not to worry, that one of the local cattle and horse-traders, Aaron Shimon, was a friend: "Tell him Chaim-Arczik [as he tended to be called in the Jewish community, in which surnames still tended to be regarded as a foreign imposition] sent you, and that I'll be in later to fix the price and pay him. Don't try to bargain with him. You just pick the horse you need and take it home. You can pay me when you harvest your crops." The man fell on his knees and started to kiss my father's hand. I didn't quite understand what it was all about at the time, but I knew my father did something good.

However naive his ideas might seem in retrospect, my father

believed in dialogue between the Jewish and Christian communities. Nor was he alone in this. Many Polish Jews, men far more important than my father, devoted lifetimes to the cause of inter-faith harmony: the name of Dr. L.L. Zamenhof, inventor of the universal language Esperanto, springs to mind as the most famous Bialystoker among them. Unfortunately, the vast majority of Christian Poles simply weren't interested in having anything to do with Jews. There was, for example, nothing in the law that said we had to live in the ghetto. It was just that the local Polish Christians would never have tolerated the physical integration of our communities. And the sad fact is that in inter-war Poland the attitudes and actions of a thousand Chaim Mielnickis would have made not one whit of difference. Of course, Wasilkow also contained its share of the more rabid type of anti-Semite (people my father always referred to as "fascists"), who absolutely hated all Jews and coveted every Jewish possession. Unfortunately, it was this latter group that seemed, to me at least, to surround the ghetto that contained Wasilkow's 1,500 Jews.

I don't know why my father didn't immigrate to the United States at the end of the First World War. I know that he was in fairly regular correspondence with his eldest brother, Isadore, in the States (all the brothers changed their name to Minick when they became American citizens, except for the one whose son, Daniel Melnick, became a well-known motion picture producer). Possibly he still resented being abandoned to his fate in Russia after the death of my grandfather in 1911. This could even be the reason why he and his brother Shmulke, and their respective families, stopped speaking to each other some time before the latter's death in the mid-1920s. It is even possible (although, I think, not probable) that Shmulke's presence in Wasilkow had nothing to do with my father's decision to settle there, and that

Chaim Mielnicki, c. 1922.

they did not speak from the outset in 1918. Those with some appreciation of the culture in which I was raised will understand that the details of this feud were never discussed or questioned in our home. But by the time I was old enough to know that I had Mielnicki cousins in Wasilkow, I somehow had been made aware that communication with these people was forbidden. (I have no idea what happened to Shmulke's wife; if she was alive when I was growing up, I have no recollection of ever having seen her.)

More probably, Chaim didn't emigrate because he didn't need to. I think that he liked the look of his prospects in a Pilsudski-led Poland. Many Jews had served in the Polish army in the fight to create an independent nation. And the fact that the Jewish Workers' Rights party (the Bund) cooperated politically with Pilsudski's Socialist Party (the *Polska Partia Socjalistyczna*) seemed to him to augur well for the future of Jews in Poland. I doubt my father actually belonged to the Bund, but he certainly had socialist inclinations. Like all Bundists, he believed that the workman deserved a fair return for his labour, and that everyone, regardless of race or religion, was entitled to his just place in this world. He was a man who always stood up and fought for the underdog. No amount of riches could ever have turned Chaim Mielnicki into a bourgeois thinker.

Most of our neighbours in Wasilkow were poor, with both husband and wife obliged to work to keep misery away from their doors, in any combination of factory jobs, textile-industry piece work, trades, crafts, carting, or small shops. And depending on whether they saw their futures in the Diaspora or in a national homeland for the Jews in Palestine, they were either Bundists, Communists, or Zionists. And talk about fight! The members of these three organizations didn't exactly kill each other, but they sure didn't like each other either. The few middle class Jews in Wasilkow, like sawmill owner Meyshke Zadwaranski (the half-dozen upper-middle-class textile mill owners lived in Bialystok), probably voted for Pilsudski, but only because his was the least anti-Semitic of the mainstream Polish political parties. Otherwise, the minor gentry in our community seemed to restrict their influence to the *Kehilla*, a local elected body, which, as I mentioned earlier, governed the purely Jewish affairs in our lives. But I digress. I would think that, in his heart, my father was both a Bundist and a Zionist, which may or may not have made him a little unusual among his peers.

———

In 1924, correctly assessing consumer demand for something more efficient than horse-drawn buses to serve local transportation needs, Chaim Mielnicki bought one of the first URSUS motor coaches (which would have been built along the lines of a contemporary North American school bus) to be manufactured in

Poland at the Zaklady Mechaniczne Ursus S.A. plant outside Warsaw. He also bought the house on Wojciechowska Street (subsequently renamed Pierwszej Brygady or First Brigade Street in Marshal Pilsudski's honour) in which my older sister and brother and I were born — a structure which extended to include a double-doored barn sufficient in size to serve as a garage and repair shop. Decisions that would seem to confirm my assertion that he intended to sink his roots in Poland. The only question was whether the Christian Poles would allow this to happen. Within a year of establishing his Express Bus Company to provide passenger and freight services between Wasilkow and Bialystok, he was forced to acquire a gentile partner named Bukhowski to escape the discriminatory licensing requirements of an increasingly corrupt and anti-Semitic civic and provincial administration.

Polonization was the order of the day in the Second Polish Republic, and, for the purposes of civil service and teaching appointments, army commissions, professional licences, university admissions, etc., Jews (even when they cut their hair, shaved their beards, dressed in Western clothing, and swore allegiance to the Polish motherland) were not considered true Poles. In Wasilkow, even the firemen now had to be Polish Christians — whereas in the past they'd all been Polish Jews. Pilsudski may have been back in power in Warsaw (he was out of politics from 1923 to 1926), but no one in Poland's capital, where the Jews now had precious little influence, seemed to give a damn about what was happening in and about Bialystok, or, in general, what was happening to the so-called "Poles with a Mosaic upbringing." (I should note that the White Russians in Wasilkow were also discriminated against by the Polish administration. "Ethnic cleansing" *per se*, however, seemed to be limited to areas with substantial Ukrainian populations.)

Fortunately, the Bukhowski-Mielnicki partnership proved a good one. They bought a second URSUS motor coach, and expanded the company's routes to encompass the many towns and villages within a thirty-kilometre radius of Bialystok. In 1926, their profits were such that my father was able to afford to buy a new Chevy, four-door touring car, with a convertible top, which must have created quite a stir in a little burg like Wasilkow, where most people didn't even have a horse and cart. Although he and Bukhowski employed full-time drivers at the Express Bus Company (we called them chauffeurs), they were very much involved in the day-to-day operation of their business. I know that my dad often collected fares, cleaned floors, fixed flats, changed the oil, and tuned the buses' Fiat engines — whatever was necessary to keep their investments bright and shiny, on the road, and running smoothly. He also drove one himself on Sundays and holidays.

Of course there was competition, and during the Great Depression this became fierce. Father and Bukhowski met this head on by working harder and longer, and then, in 1932, by lowering their Wasilkow-Bialystok fare from ten *groszy* to five (100 *groszy* equalled one *zloty*, our basic monetary unit — five *zlotys* bought one American dollar), which packed their buses to capacity, and drove their competitors to the edge of bankruptcy. In the event, my father was having a shave between runs on a Sunday morning, when someone ran into the barbershop to say that a hooligan was smashing the windows of his bus. With shaving soap still covering one side of his face, he ran out to find the burly twenty-year-old son of his principal gentile rival, lead pipe in hand, standing on the bus's front fender, trying to rip the reduced-fare sign from the inside of the broken windscreen.

Whereupon, Father pulled out the bus's crank-handle and smashed him over the back of the head, unfortunately cracking his skull. This villain was in hospital for a month and a half. And as things turned out, Father had to pay all his medical bills, and personal damages besides, to avoid going to jail for a very long time. Had the situation been reversed, however, the gentile involved, whose father had powerful political connections in Bialystok and Warsaw, would have got off scot-free. And Chaim Mielnicki, after he'd got out of hospital, where he would have had to pay his own medical bills, would have gone to jail for malicious damage to his competitor's property. Whether in consequence of this incident or not, the next year, Father found himself forced to sell his half of the business (to whom I don't know) to prevent the Express Bus Company's operating permits from being cancelled.

––––––––

It was at this juncture that my father first seriously considered emigration from Poland. His first choice, however, was Palestine, where he had some cousins, not the America of his brothers and aging mother. He obtained a visitor's visa from the British government, which held the League of Nations' mandate for this former Turkish territory, and went to investigate the possibilities for our resettlement in our historic homeland. He returned after six months, convinced that he didn't have the capital necessary to set himself up in any business worth having there; and that the alternative employment available in draining malarial swamps or breaking rock-hard soil on a kibbutz was not the answer for himself and his family. We would have to make the best of things where we were.

God knows, this was to prove a mistake of tragic proportion, but, as Father saw things, compared to Palestine, Poland seemed the better bet, despite the massive unemployment, the strikes, the demonstrations, Pilsudski's abandonment of socialist principles, and the breakdown of parliamentary democracy. Maybe it was the renewal of pogroms (if not exactly in Wasilkow, where the majority of the Christian Poles had Jewish employers, then certainly throughout the rest of the country — in August 1937 alone, there were 350 separate, *reported* attacks on Jews and Jewish businesses) that finally prompted him to apply to immigrate to the United States. But by the time he did, it was too late. Even had he been able to obtain a visa for us, it would have been too late. As my sister discovered when she received hers in 1939, the quotas were full. (Six years and six million dead Jews later, the quotas were still full.) We were caught in a web of hate from which we could not escape. But I am ahead of my story.

————

Until a few years ago, I had always imagined that my handsome father and my beautiful mother had met, courted, fallen in love, and married. My sister in Israel, however, informed me that, like almost all East European Jews of earlier generations, our parents had been introduced by a *shadchan* (marriage broker — for whom my father paid), had found each other acceptable, were married, had children, and only then had fallen in love. Looking back on what I remember of my all too short fifteen years with them, maybe there is something still to be said for competent, professional matchmakers!

————

My mother, Esther Kulecka, one of seven children (four sisters and three brothers), was born in 1903 in Michalowo, some thirty or so kilometres southeast of Bialystok. Hers was a poor, but very strict, kosher family, which had their immediate roots in Germany's Polish territories. Mother's father, whose given name and occupation I do not know, died when she was very young. Her mother, Mindl, who spent her last, bedridden months with my parents, lived until two weeks before my birth in 1927. Thus my name in her memory: Mendl (which was changed when I was four or five years old to Menachem Mendl). My mother, naturally enough, was devoted to my grandmother. Her one regret, and I'm sure something that preyed on her conscience even as her own life came to its early and lamentable end, was that she refused her mother's last request: a sour pickle. Mother didn't think anything that acidic would be good for her. Ten minutes later my grandmother was dead.

I remember my mother's family, all of whom lived in the general vicinity of Bialystok, as being very close — with the exception of one rich and rather selfish sister who owned a large bakery in Swislocz. When I was a boy, we sometimes went on vacation to her oldest brother Eli's estate in Michalowo, where I remember being greatly impressed by the orchard. A sweet and generous man (he once bought me a bright red sleigh that was the envy of all my friends), Uncle Eli had become wealthy brokering the sale of Polish agricultural products to England. When his son, my cousin Joel, who was several years older than I, came in turn to visit us, he would spend endless hours teaching me how to draw — a skill that was to prove invaluable to me when I became a fashion designer in later life. The nicest of my mother's sisters, however, was very poor. I remember that it was strictly vegetarian when I visited her in Zabludow (where two of my maternal uncles also lived). Every day I was eating potato dishes, one this way, one that way, always something different from potatoes. Married to a shoemaker, and herself the mother of three sons, she didn't have enough money to buy even the cheapest sausage, but she was always asking that I come and stay with her. But again, as with the Mielnickis, I know so little about the history of the Kulecka family that it is almost embarrassing. Not one of my maternal aunts, uncles, or cousins survived the Nazi slaughter.

As to my mother, I do know that she was only sixteen when she married my father, and that she was quite well educated for a young woman of her time. She had finished the Russian gymnasium (the equivalent of North American high school) by the time she was fourteen, and could speak Russian, Polish, Yiddish, and German. What is more, she had already worked for two years in one of the Bialystok area's many textile mills. Actually, she worked in the company store, which appears to have been a general goods

Esther Mielnicki, c. 1921.

operation designed by management to keep as large a percentage of their employees' wages as was possible from leaving the company's coffers.

Of course, like most other young women of her background and generation, she had all the skills and training necessary to establish a proper Jewish (*mikdash me-at*) home. What is more, she had learned traditional medicine at her mother's knee (and was, in time, to establish a very considerable local reputation as both a first-aid practitioner and as a healer — I particularly remember the four-litre bottle of pickled ants, from which she made pain-relieving compresses for people with arthritis). All this, in addition to being very pretty — about five-foot-four, with a petite figure, dark, sparkling eyes, and a face that was always smiling — made her quite a catch, even if she didn't have a dowry.

My sister Yente (or Lenka, as she came to be known) was born in 1920. I was still a little boy when she was already an attractive young woman, preoccupied with special soaps, lotions, and perfumes. (In later life, she became a professional beautician.) I remember that she liked to dance. I forget who organized them, but there were weekly five o'clock dances for teenagers at the hall behind the *powszechna* (Polish elementary school) — they called it "The Five" — where they danced to the sweet sounds of the Nisl Perelstein orchestra. Lenka, who was the apple of my father's eye, was never of any particular help to my mother. But then, she really didn't have to be, at least not before my father lost his bus business in 1933.

Until then, the Mielnickis were relatively rich. For example, if Mother needed help with her garden or with the washing or other household chores, she hired local peasant women. The only real demand my parents made of my sister was that she tend to her studies. And this she did, except during the six months our father was in Palestine, when, for the first time, we had to live without all the material advantages that his presence had always guaranteed.

Travelling to Palestine was an expensive business. To obtain his visitor's visa, Father had had to post a £2,000 surety bond with the British government (that he would forfeit if he didn't come back), then buy return Bialystok-Trieste-Haifa railway and passenger-ship tickets, have enough money to live on for an indefinite period, as well as to do whatever else was necessary if he decided to stay and make arrangements for us to follow. In the meantime, we had to live on what he had left us. Because we didn't know how long he would be away, this meant a very strict household budget. We certainly didn't starve, but Mother counted every *grosz*, which must have been very hard on her after the relatively high standard of living to which we'd all become accustomed. I was only five or six at the time, so what I remember most is that, when I was out with my mother, we didn't stop anymore at Lipstein's *cukiernia* (sweet shop) for a pastry, exotic fruit, or an ice cream. "Forget about it till your father comes back," she'd say, explaining that we could

MY FATHER'S SON 39

buy a two-day supply of bread for the same amount of money.

Things more or less righted themselves with Lenka after Father returned, but he had neither a steady job nor a business for the first year or two, and I don't think Lenka, whose friends came from all the "best" families, ever adapted fully to our now straitened circumstances. Certainly, she could not have been pleased when my father sold the family car (he had no choice — the authorities had refused to renew his licence until he paid taxes on the sale of his bus business). Or when he rented out the apartment that had been my nurse's to the Communist party for its Yiddish-language library, and "other activities." Although the Party was banned from seeking office or holding political rallies, opening a public library was within the law, as were the plays the Party sponsored to raise funds for political prisoners. It was whatever else they were "organizing" that made the Polish authorities nervous.

I think the government in Warsaw regarded every Polish Communist as a potential fifth columnist, and doubly so if he were Jewish. (After all, there were many former Bialystokers serving in important posts in Stalinist Russia, including Maxim Litvinov, the Soviet Commissar for Foreign Affairs.) Indeed, although there'd never been so much as a strike at any of the six Wasilkow mills, three of our local Communists (Borukh Katz, Velvl Kagan, and Khone Perlstein) were summarily arrested and imprisoned in the Polish concentration camp at Kartuzka Bereza, when it was established in 1936. So far as we were concerned, however, the only negative consequence of having the Communist party library in our house was that on certain occasions (notably May Day and the November anniversary of the Bolshevik Revolution) a policeman patrolled the front of our house, taking down the names of everyone who entered the premises, including those of Lenka's friends.

For a while, I think that Lenka may have been ashamed of us. There was, for example, the year in which we had to hide most of our household furniture in a neighbour's barn to prevent the

Polish tax collectors from seizing and selling it. Then there was the indignity that came in 1935, when Father, who was an infinitely adaptable man, bought a team of light workhorses and a wagon, and began earning his living as a carter, in competition with the likes of Uncle Shmulke's dullard second son, Yoske. Even though our father was making a decent living — one day hauling hides from the slaughter house to the local tannery, the next delivering crates of fabric from one of the local mills to the railyard in Bialystok for shipment to Russia, then waiting till eight at night to bring ten or fifteen passengers back to Wasilkow in his custom-built wagon — being the daughter of a humble carter was nothing to be proud of when your closest friend was the granddaughter of a rich butcher, and lived in a modern brick house.

However, as a little boy, I liked my sister a lot. It was my older brother Aleksei (his proper name was Aaron — in memory of my father's father, Arczik) who didn't get along with Lenka. Not that she was very nice to him. Because there were only a couple of years between them — Aleksei was born in 1922 — and because he was the eldest son and thus a potential threat to her hold on our father's affection (and her "right" always to be the only Mielnicki child to get a leg of the Shabbat-dinner chicken), Lenka seemed to go out of her way to get our brother in trouble. Often, the result was Father's belt unjustly laid across Aleksei's back and bottom, or an undeserved clip across the head with Father's cap.

Mind you, ours was still an age in which kids expected physical abuse from their parents. There was no such thing as teaching by reason, only by force, or threats: "If you do that, the Gypsies will kidnap you, keep you in chains, and make you perform like a monkey in public!" This, after all, was how our parents had been taught. And not only did no one in authority object, they thought anything less amounted to parental neglect.

Still, the situation with regard to the treatment of my siblings was unfair. Lenka, the princess, was assigned no chores at all, whereas when Aleksei, who was a genuine prince of a young man, was sent out to weed the garden, muck out the stables, feed the horses, milk the cow, whatever, there were no excuses accepted for a less than perfect job. And unlike Lenka, when my brother finished grade seven in Wasilkow, he was not sent to attend the Yiddish gymnasium on Fabryczna (Fabric) Street in Bialystok; he had to go to work with our father, hauling freight and passengers. At twelve, he had no choice but to become a man.

However, I'm sure Aleksei knew that our father, in his own way, was devoted to him as well. Father was always quick to intervene when Aleksei got into a fight with any of the neighbourhood bullies. My brother was very strong, but vulnerable: he was such a good-hearted person that he wouldn't kill a mosquito if he didn't have to. Always singing, Aleksei had a fantastic voice — like Tino Rossi, the European "Frank Sinatra" of the 1930s and '40s — a gift from God that made him irresistible to the local girls.

He was also a wonderful football striker and a powerful swimmer, until he somehow damaged his knee when he was caught in a whirlpool in the Suprasl River at Yakimes, just outside Wasilkow, where our father's Christian friend Szymanski had his flour mill. He was so pale when the men who rescued him brought him home on a stretcher that my mother thought he was going to die. (Curiously, our cow almost drowned at the very same place several years later, when the bank beneath its feet collapsed as it was drinking from the river.)

When I was little, there was no such thing in our family as buying toys. Aleksei made them for me. He enjoyed doing things for his younger brother. He even made me a wagon. It never seemed to bother him that I was five years his junior, nor that by the time I was twelve, I was taller than he was. If our mother said it was okay, he'd always let me tag along with him as he did his errands or went to visit his friends. There is no doubt that he had a profound influence on me. As I grew older, he never tired of telling me about things he thought I should know, like the Dreyfus Affair — even though he never went to high school, he was always interested in history and politics — or of encouraging me to study newspaper accounts of critical international events. I can remember, for example, when I was only ten reading all about the International Brigade in the Spanish Civil War, and keeping track of the casualties from our area.

Much later, in the Bialystok and Pruzany ghettos in 1941 and 1942, when we were working together to support our parents and sister, and then in Birkenau, when Aleksei was literally singing for our lives and our suppers, we became inseparable. I have always been my father's son, but, in many ways, my memories of Aleksei provided the model I aspired to emulate as I grew into a man. But again I am ahead of myself in recounting these events.

─────────

I was born at home on the 20th of March 1927, with the assistance of the local midwife, Prui Sternfeld, as were my sister and brother before me. Until I was five years old, I slept in a white, metal crib in the living room, outside my parents' bedroom door. Thereafter, I shared a bed with my brother. I suppose I was always a sensitive child. I remember when I was six or seven, a neighbour slammed the door on my cat, nearly cutting it in two. Of course, it had to be put out of its misery, but I was heartbroken. I cried for two or three days over its loss.

Unlike many children, my earliest memory is not about the lullabies my mother sang to me, but of a dream I had when I was maybe three years old — and one that I have had many times since, so that I know it well. In it, some extra-terrestrial force lifts me high above the earth. When I resist and want to return, it lets me loose, and I free-fall with terrifying speed straight back into my bed. Of course, the first few times this happened, I woke up screaming and crying, so much so that my mother had to rock me back to sleep, softly singing, "Sleep, my darling, / Sleep, my liebling, / Sleep, my little one, / Tomorrow will be a better day."

In the more spiritual moments of my adulthood, however, I see the forces taking me away as angels, who, when I resist, decide that I still have some duty to perform here on earth, and let me return. It's curious: although you feel as if you are being taken away from where you want to be, when your soul or spirit returns to your sleeping body, you don't feel so comfortable either. Possibly, with the completion of this book, my last responsibility on earth will be fulfilled, and if given another chance to soar beyond this vale of tears, I won't want to come back.

———

Until we lost the buses in 1933, I had a nurse. Her name was Zutka. She was a Russian, from minor aristocratic stock displaced by the Bolshevik Revolution. I don't know where her family was, but it sticks in my mind that Zutka sent her mother part of whatever my parents were paying her each month. Slim, blond, good looking, she had lots of boyfriends — even rich Jews were wanting to take her out. I was too young to be jealous, and was content always just to be snuggled against her very ample bosom. At four or five years old, I remember crying that my feet hurt when we went on walks so Zutka would pick me up and carry me. It was as if there were some kind of magnetism that pulled me to the wonder of her breasts.

Possibly this was no more than a craving for maternal affection. Then again, it may have been an early sign of a healthy male interest in the opposite sex. I know that at seven or eight, my neighbourhood pals and I were closing ourselves up in the Communist party library that had replaced Zutka in our house's apartment to examine gynaecological drawings and photographs in the medical encyclopedias. All this reminds me of the old joke

Michel Mielnicki, age twelve.

about the girl who came home from school one day and said to her mother: "Look, the boys gave me two *groszy* to stand on my head." To which her mother replied: "Silly girl, those bad boys only wanted to see your panties." "I know that, Mother," said the girl, "that's why I took them off!"

When I was ten or twelve, I would sit for hours, hidden from my mother's view in the berry bushes that hugged the fence separating our property from the one next door, my eye pressed to a knothole to watch our neighbour's twenty-year-old daughter as she sunbathed nude in their back garden. She was perhaps a little Rubenesque, but I was fascinated nevertheless. My brother told me most of what I thought I needed to know about human sexuality. (About cows and things, I already knew.) My father used to tell me too. He was a joker. Sometimes, he would see a beautiful woman walking by and say, "Now, there's a fine working machine." And I knew what he meant. This was all just part of growing up in a society that was sensual, but not promiscuous. Those girl friends that I had, I treated as colleagues, with whom one did not attempt to take liberties. Indeed, I did not lose my virginity until I returned to Bialystok after my liberation from Bergen-Belsen in 1945. But that too is another story.

———

Coming back to my nurse: once when Zutka brought me home, I had a piece of bacon in my mouth. I guess we'd gone into one of the gentile butcher shops, and she'd given me a taste. I don't remember, except that I felt so good. I was chewing it slowly, savouring the flavour, trying not to swallow it. I didn't know it was forbidden. My mother, wanting to know what I had in my mouth, fished it out with her finger. I can still hear her outraged cry: "It's *PORK!*" Did she ever give Zutka hell.

As a boy in Poland, I used to wonder why many of the Christian people always seemed so anxious to make us non-kosher or *tref.* It was as though they thought they were performing a good deed, for their side, in converting us. Not that you become less Jewish or indeed become a Christian by eating a piece of bacon. But they nevertheless felt it important to lead the Jew astray whenever they could. In fact, we didn't need their help when it came to breaking our dietary laws. Occasionally, Father would bring home some ham that had been smoked and cured by one of his gentile friends. Mother wouldn't allow it in her house, nor would she allow it to touch any of her dishes. Ignoring her disapproval, Father, Aleksei, and I would eat it off bits of wax paper in the back garden. It always tasted so delicious.

———

Our house, which, like most of its neighbours, abutted Pierwszej Brygady Street, was small by contemporary North American standards. Relative to the majority of our neighbours' houses, however, it was big. Built on a foundation of large rocks, it was constructed of planed timbers (there were only two brick houses in all of Wasilkow), and painted grey. Inside, the small apartment I've mentioned consisted of a single room, plus kitchenette — in total, some 30 to 35 feet in length, and 17 or 18 feet wide: room enough, once the Communists put shelving in, for thousands of books for all tastes and ages. The library and the Mielnicki family shared a common entrance, off the driveway at the side of the house. The doors to our separate quarters were in the vestibule, as were the stairs to our attic, in which we stored apples and other garden produce that kept well in the sawdust that served as insulation. The attic also served as an area in which to dry laundry in the winter. The large, locked cupboard in which Mother stored her various medicinal herbs and potions, as well as large sacks of flour and salt, sat under the stairs.

Our door opened into the kitchen, which was very efficient in design, made to measure for Mother. It had a window facing the street (shuttered to keep out the rocks when the Christian fanatics went on a rampage), half-windowed double-doors leading into the large living room/dining room area, and, on the remaining wall, the doorway into the children's bedroom (Lenka's portion was curtained off from that shared by Aleksei and me). It also had a trapdoor which provided access to the cellar, where we kept our potatoes, turnips, parsnips, carrots, big white onions, garlic, barrels of pickles and sauerkraut, preserved fruit, jams, marmalades, beets, beans, and tomatoes. One of my jobs was trapping the rats that all these good things attracted. (And I guess it was a good thing for me that my mother never discovered that I sometimes drowned these rodents in the rainwater she collected for washing her hair.) Our parents' bedroom, as I've mentioned, was off the living room. The two wood-burning ovens in the kitchen and the brazier in the front room provided our heat.

Because every house I was ever in as a boy had red floors, I

The Mielnicki home in Wasilkow.

don't think I ever thought to ask anyone why ours were painted red as well: they simply were — and repainted every two or three years. The ceilings were wooden, but painted white, or light grey, or pale yellow: colours to reflect a maximum of light. Except for the kitchen, the walls were papered in attractive floral or paisley patterns. We ate our breakfasts by the window in the kitchen dinette. Dinner was always served at our beautiful big dining room table, which, when it was not lit by *Shabbat* or festival candles, was illuminated by Mother's sparkling chandelier. The rest of the front room was comfortably and tastefully furnished as well — lace curtains over a second, street-side, shuttered window, hand-crafted rugs, over-stuffed chesterfield and chairs, beautifully inlaid occasional tables, chests, sideboards: that sort of thing.

I remember that a large photo-portrait of my parents hung on one of the walls. And on another, a painting of the temptation of Adam and Eve that Father brought back from Palestine. Exquisitely done, I wish I had it today — it's probably hanging in some gentile's living room, or in one of their churches. Oh yes, there was also a big, gilt-framed mirror in the dining area. And cactuses (aloe vera): Mother had at least half a dozen of them, the juice of which she used for treating burns and infected cuts. We didn't have a piano or a gramophone, and the first radio we had was the two-tube one (powered by an eight-cell car battery) that I made at school in 1940. More important though, our house had a warm and inviting atmosphere — Mother and Father created that with their sense of hospitality. On Saturdays, when people came to visit, there was always the glass of hot tea, served Russian-style with a spoonful of marmalade or jam.

On other occasions, the drink was stronger. Father liked his vodka, and always kept a jug of overproof on top of a shelf in the kitchen. I'd been allowed to taste Mother's homemade beer and kosher wine (even to the point of occasionally falling asleep at the table from its effects), but vodka, never. Home alone one day when I was seven or eight, I decided to investigate its properties. To reach my objective, I had to put a chair on the dinette table. As that first fiery mouthful seared my throat I lost my balance and flew backwards, the large glass jug clutched in both my hands. Fortunately for life and limb, I landed on the cushioned bench alongside the table. The important thing, or so I thought at the time, was that I hadn't let a drop of vodka spill. My interest in hard drink, however, ended once I returned the container to its accustomed place.

Father's didn't. If he had been visiting with his Russian or Polish Christian friends, he might arrive home entirely the worse for wear. To my mother's horror and loud complaint, as I recall, he once staggered into the living room, unbuttoned his fly, and peed against the wall. Another time, when I was helping my mother steam off the wallpaper in our front room, I found a bullet hole underneath. "What is this doing here?" I asked. She told me that before I was born there'd been a party where my father, in a burst of wild, and no doubt drunken enthusiasm, took out his pistol and fired a shot into the wall to wake up one of the guests. What a guy! He was very much his own man, and also very demanding. But this was not a problem for my mother, who had her own opinions on most things, and was not shy about expressing them.

————

A common red clay tiled roof extended from our house to the attached barn, which contained stables for our horses and cow (as well as her yearly calf), a roost for our chickens, geese, and turkeys, my dad's workshop, with its gigantic wall of tools (all of them fascinating to a small boy, who could hardly wait until he was old enough to try them out), and, after we lost our buses and car, ample storage for Father's wagon and carriage. There was, of course, a hayloft above, in which my friends and I loved to jump and roll about, despite my mother's warnings about the dangers involved. "Don't lie down in the hay or you'll fall asleep and die!" Once we even had a goat. He kept unwanted guests off the property, but he also ate everything in sight.

————

Three feet behind the barn was the outhouse, which was a fair run from our front door, especially in the wintertime. I remember the dark and stormy night that my sister, in a mad dash through the deep and drifting snow to reach this facility, lost a new pair of slippers with big red, feather pompons on the toes, which we didn't find again until the snow melted. Of course, like everyone else in Wasilkow, we had to make arrangements to have the pit cleaned out twice a year. And, in January and February, given the extra traffic from the Communist library, we had to hire someone to come with an axe and chop away the frozen excess that threatened to stab anyone who sat down. Mother always planted a great number of flowers around the outhouse in the spring and summer in the vain hope that they would somehow mask its all-pervasive odour with their perfume.

———

Mother's kitchen garden, which was, maybe, two hundred feet long by fifty or sixty feet wide, took up the rest of our lot. If I close my eyes, I can still see where everything was planted, row upon row: potatoes on the right side, cabbage on the left, with corn and sunflowers down the middle, and the rest of the vegetables and herbs in their complementary places. Her garden was so successful (tomatoes that weighed a pound, onions four inches in diameter) that she was able to start her own seed business. (Each year in her memory, I plant a few string beans in my flower garden here in Vancouver.) And when I grew old enough, I was placed in charge of selling the vegetables we didn't need for ourselves — money that was used to buy my school supplies.

I also took my turn at milking our very nice red cow, and in delivering her surplus production to several of our neighbours. I should note that because we had no land on which our cow could graze, during those months when pasture was available, she joined the other ghetto cattle each morning in a parade through the streets of Wasilkow and into the countryside beyond. This was done under the supervision of the *pastuch*, or peasant cowherd, who would bring them back in time for their evening milking. Each cow knew where she belonged and would leave the herd of her own accord when she reached her yard.

———

We didn't have running water. Nor did the well, which we shared with several neighbours, have a pump. We drew our water up by the

Wasilkow's Synagogue Square.

bucketful, which meant a lot of work, especially on laundry days. For washing woolens and other things that required soft water, Mother used the rainwater we collected. Interestingly, a town ordinance banned rain barrels from the street-side of the houses. Another bylaw required all homeowners to remove any grass growing through the cobblestones on the street in front of their houses — twice a year we hired some unemployed gentile to sit on the street and do this with a knife. Yet another demanded street-side window boxes filled with flowers. I don't know how these regulations were applied in the Christian sections of our town, where, for example, the streets were dirt, but, ironically, when the German army reached our doors in 1939 and 1941, the Jewish part of Wasilkow looked like something out of a Bavarian village.

––––––––

I wouldn't say our family was overly religious. Like everyone else in our community, we went on Saturdays to the synagogue to which we belonged (which was one of four in Wasilkow, member-ship being determined by economic status) and to the Great Shul (which everyone attended regardless of means) on high holidays. My brother and I went to *cheder*, where we studied under Rebbe Shmul Batlai (who didn't hesitate to clout us vigorously when we made a mistake in one of our lessons), and were respectively *bar mitzvahed* when we reached the age of thirteen. A rabbinical student had taught my sister such as she needed to know in terms of household prayers and blessings.

My father, however, given his experiences in the Great War, probably sometimes questioned the very existence of God, although he did not make a point of proclaiming this. Indeed, although he paid to maintain our membership in the Beth Amidrash Synagogue, I don't recall that he spent much time discussing religious matters at all. Certainly, he ate non-*kosher* meals outside the house, and might well have preferred life in a secular society had this been possible; in that sense, he would have been better off in America. He was what you might call a "progressive" Jew. I know he thought the Hasidic members of our community, who preferred prayer to hard work, peculiar in the extreme.

Still, I also think that he found comfort in our traditions. For example, when he received word that his mother had died in New York on the second day of Passover in 1939, I remember him rending his vest, removing his shoes, and sitting *shivah* (mourning) on a low wooden stool, according to the requirements of our religion. (Actually, my mother had kept his brother's telegram from him for a day so as not to spoil the high holiday, which was of course the proper thing to do.) Certainly, he was a good man, who took great pleasure in helping other people, whether Jew or gentile, when he could.

Mitzvah finds its definition in *Psalms* 119:35, which says, "Direct me in the path of Your *mitzvot*, for I delight in it." Earlier, I told the story of my father buying a new horse for the gentile peasant. As I later discovered, Father got a good price on the horse, carried the loan, and didn't charge the man a *grosz* of interest. (You're not supposed to make money on a good deed.) One *mitzvah*, of course, encourages the next. Later, when this Christian came to settle his debt, he not only paid in full, he brought us gifts of honey, and butter, and eggs, and all kinds of things.

In 1979, the Committee on Reform Jewish Practice published *Gates of Mitzvah, A Guide to the Jewish Life Cycle*. In it, they described *mitzvah* as "the key to authentic Jewish existence and to the sanctification of life. No English equivalent can adequately translate the term. Its root meaning is 'commandment,' but *mitzvah* has come to have broader meanings. It suggests the joy of doing something for the sake of others and for the sake of God, and it conveys still more: it also speaks of living Jewishly, of meeting life's challenges and opportunities in particular ways. All this is *mitzvah*."

In that sense, it comes very close to my understanding of *kashrut*. My mother, for example, was very much about the business of organizing food, clothing, and firewood for the poor (and there were lots of them in our community). A saint some people called her for her good works, but she was brought up to be a follower of the *kashrut*. *Kashrut*, which, of course, encompasses our dietary laws, also means everything Jewish, in the sense of following a line, a pattern in life. So you don't go sideways, where you're not supposed to.

The fact is, however, that the social/religious aspects of life in the ghetto were self-regulating to such a high degree that going astray was difficult. We lived cheek by jowl with our neighbours. In consequence, everybody knew a great deal about everybody else's business, to the extent that no one could escape unnoticed if they broke the fundamental taboos and requirements that bound us as a people. And despite what I said earlier about political divisions, in the final analysis, we were all Jews. If the men sometimes lost sight of this, the women, whose charitable works and general prattle encompassed the entire community, did not.

In extreme cases, an individual might be excommunicated by

the rabbi. In Wasilkow, our chief rabbi was Israel Halpern, a very learned and much respected man. *The Wasilkower Memorial Book* by Leon Mendelewicz cites the example of Rabbi Halpern excommunicating a Jewish Communist who refused to have his new son circumcised. And I remember the case of a young Jewish woman being excommunicated after she'd aborted yet a second child conceived with a gentile policeman. In the old days, the rabbis were our judges, our psychiatrists, everything. The Jewish people didn't go to the public courts or professional counsellors if they had disputes or problems. They went to the rabbi, and they accepted his decision.

More commonly, an errant individual would be ostracized by his father or by the community at large. For example, my cousin Yosel (Shmulke's eldest son) lived with a gentile woman, with whom he had an illegitimate son in 1931 or 1932. Because we didn't associate with them, I don't know what happened exactly, but in a normal Jewish family Yosel would have been disowned. It is ironic, I suppose, that because this child of Yosel's was his mother's son and a Catholic with a Slavic name, he was the only member of Uncle Shmulke's family to escape the Holocaust. All the rest were murdered at Treblinka.

On a happier note: I remember the various Jewish holidays of my childhood as pure delight. The food was different. It was better. Special. And plentiful. All the adults were good to you, because everybody was in a fine humour and relaxing. You would play chestnuts (like marbles) or trade military buttons (we collected sets of buttons from the uniforms of the various Polish regiments as well as those of foreign armies) with the other kids in the square surrounding the Great Shul and the synagogues (Shul Place, or Synagogue Square as it more often was called). *Purim* was like a North American Halloween. You dressed up and knocked on the neighbourhood doors, saying, "*Purim* is today. Give us a few *groszy* and we will go away."

At *Passover*, your parents bought you a new suit of clothes and squeaky new shoes. (The joke was that your shoes squeaked only if they weren't paid for.) One of Wasilkow's more specialized seasonal industries was making matzah to meet some of the *Passover* needs of the much larger Jewish community in Bialystok. And because I was from a good family (being very *kosher*), Berl-Jacob Moses'es, the cantor at the Great Shul and one of the supervisors of our matzah production, allowed me to pour the water into the flour, which was not only an immense honour, but a task that always earned me a couple of kilos of walnuts as a reward.

At *Hanukkah*, the eight nights of candle lighting to celebrate the rededication of the Temple by the Maccabees following their victory over the Syrians more than two thousand years ago, you received gifts. I loved it because I was getting a dollar or two from every uncle in the United States. We used to call these greenbacks the *Logschen* (the green macaroni). I was thinking: "Why can't we have a holiday all the time?"

The steam bath for the Jewish community in Wasilkow was just three houses away from where we lived. Until I was old enough to go with my father, my bathing took place in a tin tub in the kitchen, or with a bar of soap and a cloth from the wash basin. Certainly, we were nowhere near as personally hygienic as we are today with hot and cold running water, and bathtubs and showers in every house, but we were cleaner than the average gentile. The rules dictated that the men and the women of our community attend the steam bath separately. They also demanded that this facility be thoroughly scoured after the females departed their *mikvahs* (ritual baths at the completion of their menstrual cycles).

To me, the steam bath was its own occasion: a communal rite of individual purification before we went to our synagogues that further served to bind us. Besides, nothing that I know of makes a man feel so wonderfully clean as the copious perspiration the steam bath's blinding heat inspires in an otherwise thoroughly washed and rinsed body. I remember thinking I would die the first time Father put me up on the highest bench. Sad to say, I have no stories of heroics around our steam bath comparable to that of my father and his friends in Rzhev. Apparently, a bunch of them liked to come out of the steam bath, jump into the Volga River through a hole they'd cut in the ice, climb out, roll in the snow, then restart their circulation with a bottle of vodka as they ran back to the bath house. The Jews of Wasilkow were a rather staid lot by comparison.

———

Talking about ice: we had no Frigidaires or iceboxes. During the late fall or early spring, or in the winter, when the temperature sometimes dropped to eighteen below, we didn't need them. But for the other six months of the year the Jewish community had a big underground icehouse not far from Synagogue Square. Beginning in February, Polish and White Russian peasants would arrive with wagon loads of metre-and-a-half-long blocks of ice that they had cut with handsaws in the local lakes and rivers. These would be covered with sawdust and ground up corn husks to retard the melting process, then stacked until the place was full. And every butcher (there were half a dozen) or family that wanted one could rent its own locker in which to store meat throughout the summer months.

———

I don't recall our ever having had one of these lockers. What would we have stored in it? Such meat as we normally bought was in the winter or early spring when vegetables were scarce. Then, Mother would buy from Shmulke Perelstein's wife, Rachel (a big, strong woman in her early fifties, who handled the sales for the only butcher in town rich enough to have his own icehouse), whatever she was going to cook that day. But no more. If we were having chicken for *Shabbat* dinner, as we usually did, it had to be killed by the *shochet*, our ritual slaughterman, Friday morning. The fact, however, was that we simply were not great beef or mutton eaters. Besides, *kosher* meat, because it had to be rendered veinless by our butchers, was expensive (about three or four times what the gentiles paid for theirs) — a kilo cost three *zlotys*, the equivalent of a day-and-a-half's minimum wages .

When I reflect fondly on my first memories of my mother's cooking, images of heavily salted, boiled meat never come to mind. Instead, my mouth will water at the thought of how delicious the buttermilk tasted after I'd helped with the churning. Or I'll think of *tzimmes*, a slow-baking casserole made from carrots or parsnips or turnips and honey: something better you've never experienced — like Hawaiian passion fruits. I don't know how the word "*tzimmes*" came also to mean "fuss," or "uproar," or "big deal" among Jews, but I would never make such a *tzimmes* over missing a prime rib dinner. However, sauerkraut, warmed in a little oil, then mixed with mashed potatoes, was something I fantasized about as a half-starved inmate in Birkenau, or as I lay at death's door too weak from hunger even to move from my bunk when the British army liberated Bergen-Belsen in April 1945.

And borscht! I dreamed of borscht. And schav — like borscht, except made from spinach or sorrel, with a spicy taste. Cooked and cooled, and mixed with sour cream, then garnished with thin slices of cucumber, radish, and hardboiled egg, and served with black bread: these were among our summertime delicacies. Or, in the spring, wild yellow mushrooms fried in butter, then mixed with scrambled eggs. I loved that. And, of course, gefilte fish (Russian style, with salt and carrots and lots of onions). Or chicken liver, or Mother's very special chopped goose liver. Or even just a piece of freshly baked bread, spread with some of our home-manufactured cream cheese (a little business that my father started on the side in 1938), and topped with a slice of raw white onion. But enough.

———

The point is not that my mother, like everybody else's mother, was the world's greatest cook, or that being subjected to a starvation diet for almost four years in situations of unparalleled brutality adds poignancy to every memory of childhood love and comfort, of which food is such an important part, but that I credit the relative absence of meat from my early diet for giving me the physical strength to survive the death camps. In my observation, of that small percentage of inmates who somehow managed to endure Birkenau and other such places, the overwhelming majority began with strong, solid, sinewy bodies. The fat ones quickly died.

Lest I be misunderstood, my point, such as it is, is that *kosher* kitchens help make good Jews, but not necessarily ones with bodies healthy enough to survive a famine. Of course, I am pre-occupied with the question of how, or more particularly, why I, Michel Mielnicki, survived the Holocaust, when millions of my Jewish brothers and sisters did not. Almost every survivor asks the same of him or herself, and continually searches, albeit often in a seemingly endless series of anecdotal digressions, for answers that can never be found.

———

Survival, of course, has been a Jewish preoccupation since time immemorial. In 1939 and '41, it was the scale and nature of the Nazi assault on our existence that was new. When I was a boy in Wasilkow, death stalked our ghetto streets every day. The difference was that the murders were most often random and individual, not organized and collective. For example, my sister's girlfriend Hannah Gotlieb ("Shmulke the Butcher" Perelstein's grand-daughter) had a brother-in-law, a weightlifter named Yankel, who was killed right in front of her house one day by a drunken gentile, who pulled out a knife, and stabbed him in the back, piercing his heart. Of course, this man was arrested, charged, tried, and sentenced to a few years in jail, but to murder a so-called "Christ-killer" was never that much of a big deal in the land of the Black Madonna.

Before I went to *cheder* when I was six, I didn't know much about Christ. I thought he was a Polack, because the gentiles always said, "You killed our Christ." I've often thought that these Polish anti-Semites might have thought and acted a little differently had they been told by their priests (the Roman Catholic Church has a lot to answer for) that Christ was himself a Jew, a rabbi to boot, and undoubtedly circumcised. But, from what I saw and heard, the Christian Poles were generally an ignorant lot, especially the peasants (two-thirds of the population were dependent on agricultural production), who believed whatever they were told about us, including myths about Jews stealing Christian babies so that we could make matzah with their blood.

This, of course, didn't stop these people lusting after our young women. "To hell with the Jew, but love to the Jewess" is the polite translation of what was, before the War at least, a common Polish gentile expression. This sentiment was not reciprocated, however. Unaccompanied, their women were certain to go unmolested in our communities. Ours had no such guarantee in theirs.

In Wasilkow, Jewish girls and boys learned from a very early age that none of our streets was perfectly safe, and that there were parts of our small town (which, in total, was hardly more than three main roads and a few dozen side streets) that we entered at our peril — where no policeman would come to our aid, whatever the offence. We didn't live in constant terror of the gentiles, but we tended to confine our social and other activities to the ghetto where we lived, which was centred on Shul Place, and exercised due caution when we ventured forth, even to school.

For example, my mother always walked my sister back and forth to school when she attended the *powszechna*. It was only about eight minutes from our front door, but five of them were in "enemy territory." When I began school, Aleksei was in grade six, and I walked with him. My brother was no street fighter, but he'd earned a certain respect as an athlete. When Aleksei went to work with Father after grade seven, however, I had to learn to dodge the stones that were thrown at me every afternoon as I ran the two blocks from the school to the safety of our ghetto.

That is, until my father bought me a large, cross-bred Dalmatian guard dog, called "Suchart," that he trained to meet me after school. This kept the Christian bullies at their distance, but it didn't solve my problems during recess and lunch hour. I don't know how Lenka and Aleksei survived their particular situations, but I discovered that I could buy protection — that there were always three or four gentile boys who were prepared to be my "friends" if I gave them one of my mother's freshly baked cookies in return for taking my side whenever any quarrel developed. My poor mother could never figure out how I could possibly eat the number of cookies I took each day, and I never told her the truth.

On one occasion — I forget now whether it was because my dog didn't show up or because I didn't have any cookies that day — I arrived home covered in blood. One of the older boys had hit me in the forehead with a small rock. This must have been in 1935, otherwise my father wouldn't have been around to come to my aid. I would have been eight years old. In any event, Father marched me right back to the *powszechna* so that I could point out my assailant, which I did. Whereupon, he grabbed that fat slob by the nose with two fingers and gave it such a twist that it swelled to double its size.

Unfortunately, the school principal saw this, and had my father charged with common assault. Chaim Mielnicki was found guilty by the local magistrate, and sentenced to two weeks in jail. The funny thing was that under Polish law, he didn't have to serve the sentence himself. For minimum wages (two *zlotys* a day), he hired an unemployed gentile, who went to jail in his stead. I know this to be a fact, because I had to bring this fellow his lunch every day — which was part of the bargain. This guy never ate so good in all his life. After two weeks, he was out looking for a job again. He said that he wished my father had received a longer sentence.

I don't think that I would have dared to complain about this to my father or mother — I would have received a hit across the ear for my trouble — but relative to the Christian kids with whom I went to school, I thought my young life in Wasilkow unfairly restricted. Jewish parents are very protective. I was allowed to go to plays and concerts, or to see the occasional silent movie at the *Dom Ludowy* (People's Hall), which was really just a big empty barn, if I was accompanied by my brother or my mother. Or sometimes we would all go into Bialystok for a show. But when it came to things that I really wanted to do, it was a different story.

There was a lake, not more than a twenty-minute walk from our house, where everybody skated and played hockey in the wintertime, but my parents refused to buy me a pair of skates, so I wouldn't break a leg. Similarly, even though there was very little high-speed traffic on the streets of Wasilkow, or on the road to Bialystok for that matter, they never bought me a bike because somebody else's child broke an arm falling off a bike. When I looked at my gentile classmates, I thought: "They don't need their parents always to supervise everything they do. They can swim when they want to. They can eat this. They can go there. They don't even have to do their homework. We are the same as these people, why should we be treated so differently?"

Where the Christians seemed to me to play all the time and take life for granted, we did not. We had to prepare for our future. For example, we couldn't go out and play if we hadn't done our homework. Their attitude was, "Who cares?" Until the next day, of course, when, naturally enough, we were the ones who answered all the questions at school. Then there was jealousy and resentment on the part of our gentile colleagues, which made our lives all the more difficult. I'm not suggesting that the Jews of Wasilkow were all educated, or even literate. (My mother wrote letters for lots of people in our community who couldn't read or write — this she also did as a *mitzvah*.) What I am saying is that most Jewish parents thought differently from their Polish Christian counterparts about education.

History had taught Jewish people that they couldn't afford to become attached to any country, in the sense of believing that they were going to be there forever. When you live in places where there's an ever-present danger you'll be annihilated — where a change of government may result in someone taking away your business, your house, your bread, your life — your thinking is bound to be different from those whose culture has not been shaped by the knowledge that they might have to flee at any moment. Consequently, Jews tended to regard education as a form of easily transportable wealth, like diamonds, or gold, or rare stamps. So if their kids had a brain, they sent them to school, and demanded they succeed, as some small guarantee against an uncertain future. And given a so-called traditional family structure, this meant that the mother, rather than the father, became the driving force behind her children's success at school. Certainly,

A typical pre-war Jewish orchestra.

this was the case in the Mielnicki household.

I remember coming home at the end of one school year when I was eight or nine with a bare pass in Polish. My mother was not pleased. She made such a *tzimmes* over my poor mark that I started crying. I think she even gave me a cuff, which was something she rarely did. Maybe she was just having a bad day, but the whole thing upset me so much, I couldn't stop crying. I just lay on the chesterfield and bawled my eyes out. My nerves were so completely frazzled that I tore my report card in half. I think my mother should have calmed me. Instead, she ignored me, and I felt that something deep inside me had been destroyed. This one incident, however, is the only bad memory I have of her, and I record it here because it seems significant of the damage that parents, however well intentioned, can do when they make their love conditional on some level of achievement by their children.

————

Yiddish was the *lingua franca* of our community. Although there were regional variations — we spoke a Lithuanian/Russian dialect — this was the common language of European Jewry, and my mother made sure that my sister, brother and I could read and write it before we went into the Polish school system. I should note that because Yiddish is a phonetic and syntactically simple language, it is easy for even a child to master. It also didn't hurt that the Communist party had its Yiddish library in our house. I don't think my father ever took a book out, but my mother did. She liked the romances.

Naturally, I began with the illustrated children's books, and progressed from there to stories by Sholem Aleichem (on which the famous musical *Fiddler on the Roof* is based) and books by Sholem Asch (*The Witch of Castile*), to more political things like Emile Zola's open letter, *J'accuse*, and accounts of the Spanish Civil War. What really interested me, however, were the technical manuals on mechanics and electricity, which became my passion as I made experiments, often to the delight of my schoolmates (both Christian and Jewish) at my father's wonderful workbench. This doesn't mean that I always understood everything I was reading, but the more you read, the more questions you ask, the more you learn. By the time I was twelve, I'd started my own little business repairing electrical appliances.

————

Of course, the Mielnicki children were multilingual. In addition to Yiddish, we could all speak Polish, Russian, and German before we entered grade one. And, over the years, I have added French, English, and Spanish to my repertoire. In thinking about my own experience with languages, however, I have come to believe that the ruling classes in many countries conspired to make their languages inordinately difficult in order to prevent the average Joe from mastering them. The aristocrats and bourgeois businessmen, who knew good French, or good English, or good German, used their knowledge to consolidate their wealth and power, whereas the lower classes, because they couldn't read and write with any degree of skill, if at all, were kept in economic servitude. When Lenin came to power in Russia, he immediately reformed the language: the New Russian, they called it. Why, I have often asked, can't this be done with French or English or German today? Or with Polish, or Hungarian, or with any other language for that matter?

––––––

In any event, my formal education began in 1932, when I was five years old, when my parents enrolled me in kindergarten at the Sholem Aleichem School, which was a private Yiddish elementary school. The next year, however, because it fit my father's integrationist philosophy, I began the first of my six years at the Polish state elementary school (*powszechna*), where I was one of a mere handful of Jewish students — the majority attended either Sholem Aleichem or Yavneh (formerly Tachkemoni) College, the Hebrew school. When the Soviets took over in 1939, I was sent to begin grade seven at the high school in Bialystok. Because the language of instruction in our schools was now changed to Russian, in which I, unlike most of my schoolmates, was fluent, I found myself able to complete three years in two. I don't know if the Christian kids continued to go to school after the German invasion of June 1941, but this event certainly brought an end to my academic career.

Still, such as it was, mine had been a pretty intensive educational program, and no more so than at the elementary level, where after finishing at the *powszechna* in the early afternoon, the Jewish boys and girls attended Sholem Aleichem for two hours of

Yiddish language and literature classes, while the gentiles stayed behind to do their one hour of Roman Catholic prayers and catechism. My formal religious instruction until age twelve took place Monday through Thursday, after dinner, when I attended *cheder*. After that, until my *bar mitzvah*, the rebbe gave me private lessons (during which he sometimes fell asleep when I was reading aloud). Then, Friday, at four, the Sabbath started, so there wasn't much time for sleighs and snowballs, except on Sundays. No wonder, as a kid, I thought I was hard done by.

The *powszechna* wasn't a big school: maybe two hundred students and half a dozen instructors. My favourite teacher was a Russian who taught us science and mathematics. Like my father, he had not returned home after the Revolution. I remember that he would play his violin while we were doing our assignments. A fantastic player. He also had a very pretty wife. What really interested me though was that he had a motorcycle, which he occasionally allowed me to wash and shine. Once, he even let me help him take apart the engine. And sometimes, he would give me a hair-raising ride to Bialystok, where he would buy me a piece of ham or *kielbasa* (beef and pork sausage with lots of garlic) as a special treat (I didn't tell my mother). Maybe he liked me because he too experienced discrimination at the hands of the Polish government. Because he was a Russian, he was not allowed to teach in Bialystok or any other large centre, where the law required that all the teachers be Polish nationals. He could teach only in the small towns and villages, and then only if there wasn't some Pole, other than a Jew, who wanted his job.

In fact, however, I got on well with all my teachers, even the one who taught me Polish, who seemed to understand that the root of my problem lay in a confusion of the several languages I had learned at too early an age. In physical education, which was compulsory, I excelled, like my brother before me, in soccer and volleyball. Our sports teacher was also in charge of the Polish Army Cadet Corps for ten- to twelve-year-olds — sort of Boy Scouts with rifles, but future officers nonetheless. I desperately wanted to join, to be a soldier like my father, but they didn't allow Jews, *by law*, even though they'd take us into the army as cannon fodder when we were of age.

————

Still, as a boy, I didn't hate the Christian Poles. I may have given the impression that my life at school was one of constant harassment. It wasn't. I accepted the anti-Semitic bullying, when it occurred (which wasn't every day), as something I had to deal with as best I could. I learned how to trade insult for insult. When some gentile said, "*Sukisyn*" (son of a bitch), I replied, "*Skurwysyn*" (son of a slut). If he said, "Hitler's going to come and fix you dirty Jews," I rejoined, "Go back to where you came from inside your mother." But I didn't spit on the ground at the sight of a Roman Catholic nun, as some Jews did. My father would have beaten me silly if he'd ever caught me doing such a thing.

And I didn't think to condemn all Christians for worshipping a false messiah and his mother. Quite the contrary, I thought their Christmas a wonderful celebration, and was happy to make decorations in art class for the school Christmas tree, and to help trim it with the other kids. I knew the words to all their Christmas carols, and blithely sang along in music class and assembly. What is more, I loved it when my father hitched up the horse and sleigh to take the neighbourhood children and me through the gentile sections of Wasilkow on a winter's eve at Christmastime (which was celebrated according to both the Julian and Gregorian calendars, depending whether the household in question was Polish Roman Catholic or White Russian Orthodox).

Father had a special harness with little bells on it that he put on the horse, and we'd jingalingalingaling along, marvelling at the decorations on the windows, and the trees all lit with burning candles that we could see inside the houses. The highlights were the elaborate nativity scenes outside the Catholic and Orthodox churches.

A shtetl funeral procession.

Another treat came when he took me to visit the home of Mr. Bogucki, the director of the power generating station, who was a good friend of his. (It was not uncommon for a successful Polish Christian to have somewhere in the background a good Polish Jew who was giving him ideas with which to get ahead in life.) Now, this man had a tree that everybody in our town talked about, because it was the only one to be decorated with strings of blinking electric light bulbs. The very sight of this wondrous curiosity made me think that maybe I'd been born into the wrong religion.

I also remember, as a boy, each year at Easter delivering parcels of homemade *kosher* wine and matzah to the mayor of Wasilkow, the police chief, and various of their cronies. My father, I guess, considered this an important public relations gesture. You know, "In case I sometime need a favour from you gentile guys."

Before the German invasion, the crowning indignity in our lives happened in the summer of 1939. That August, with Mrs.

Sternfeld again in attendance, my mother gave birth to her fourth child, a son, two months premature. I can still visualize him lying all bundled and warm, so tiny and sweet in his little bassinet. It was beyond my comprehension that he should die after just two days of life, but I think my mother knew he would. Of course, both baby and mother should have been transferred immediately to the Jewish Hospital in Bialystok. There were no incubators in Wasilkow, and no practising physicians. But this is not the point of the story.

When my father, brother, and our rabbi went to bury my baby brother in the local Jewish cemetery, which was three or four kilometres outside town, they discovered that it was being used as part of a training ground by units of the Polish Army. Armed sentries barred their entry. They were told that the cemetery was off limits to civilians because the exercise in progress involved the use of live ammunition. The indignant protests of our rabbi made not the least impression on the Polish officer in charge. So my father had to turn the horse and carriage around, come back through Wasilkow, and beyond to a 300-year-old Jewish cemetery, long since fallen into disrepair. (Jews had lived in Wasilkow for over 500 years.) There, they dug a grave, made the prayers, buried that little body, a white blanket for its shroud, and marked his spot with a small headstone.

Two days later, a peasant knocked on our door and asked to see my father. "Sir Mielnicki," he said, "some people must have thought you were burying gold in the old cemetery, because they've dug up the grave, and left your baby where they dropped it when they ran away." My father, for all his experience in life, was shocked — stunned — devastated. "How could anyone do such a thing?" he asked, almost in a whisper. This was no mere personal affront, but one to God and all things Jewish (and Christian as well). Then anger filled him, and he answered, "These savages!" There were no words, not even our rabbi's, to comfort him.

But it was no uneducated peasant who shortly thereafter informed the quartermaster of the Polish cavalry regiment camped nearby that the loft of our barn was filled with hay, and that we had a team of good light horses, with the consequence that both feed and horses were summarily requisitioned, as was Father's custom-built wagon — no doubt, although I have no specific memory of this, all properly receipted (as legal robberies normally are). At that point, anticipating the worst, we put all the family silver and other valuables (even my mother's fur coat) into a large wooden box and buried it beneath the dirt floor of our barn. I remember my father making certain that the lid of our packing case was more than a bayonet-length beneath the surface, reflecting his own experience in searching for caches of arms, food, or hidden loot during the First World War. The irony here is not lost on me, but the critical point remains that the outbreak of World War II found the Mielnicki family without much left to lose, and ready to flee for their lives.

CHAPTER II

DAYS OF BLISS AND HORROR

What I remember most about the first few days of what has since come to be known as World War II was the ordinance that required us to paste widths of paper diagonally across our windows to prevent their shattering in an air attack. Of course, I was only twelve years old when the German army crossed the Polish frontier on 1 September 1939. And in our small town of Wasilkow, we had no accurate sources of information about what was happening at the front (as it turned out there were a number of them), or even where these fronts were. Nor did we know what effect the immediate British and French declarations of war on Germany would have — that is, when we finally heard about them on 5 September. (None, as it turned out.)

And no one, my ex-cavalryman father included, could have anticipated the devastating effect of the German *Blitzkrieg* upon the Polish armed forces. Initially, apart from blackout restrictions, the occasional air raid on the Bialystok railyards (which, among other things, destroyed the train station), and roads jammed with military transport (which included horse-drawn peasant carts and vintage World War I army trucks with solid rubber tires that travelled at about ten kilometres per hour maximum), we seemed far away from whatever was happening.

The one exception during the first week of the War was a dog-fight over Wasilkow between a Polish P.Z.L. fighter and a Messerschmitt 109. When their air-duel took them into the cloud cover behind a nearby hill, my father borrowed our neighbour's saddle horse, and galloped out to watch whatever there was to see. Other excited and curious townsfolk followed him on foot, each desperately hoping to witness a Polish victory. They were still hurrying to catch up to Father when the scream of an engine and the sound of a crash told them the outcome had been decided. Blithely confident of no less a result than the one they wished for, they cheered, only to be strafed a second later by the German raider.

In the meantime, Father raced his horse to the aid of the downed pilot, whose plane, on being hit by his opponent's heavy calibre machine guns, had taken a nosedive into the soft earth of a farmer's newly ploughed field. He found the young airman still strapped to his seat, with part of his head blown away and his brains hanging out. There being nothing Father could do to help, he turned his horse homeward to inform the municipal authorities, so that they could take charge of the scene before it was looted by enterprising peasants. What struck my twelve-year-old mind as curious in my father's account as he related it to us a little later was that the only items to have been dislodged in the crash were the pilot's papers, including his wallet, which had somehow spilled from the now open cockpit onto the ground below.

In any event, by late afternoon, the downed plane had been hauled behind the high wooden fence of the Wasilkow municipal gardens, where it sat, hidden from public view except when the gates to the gardens opened to let the workmen in or out — at which point, nearby adults and children strained for a glimpse of this bizarre testament to the dashed expectations of the local populace. This in itself may have been appropriate, because even as the thunder of German artillery drew closer, and wounded

Polish soldiers with bandaged heads and arms began to fill the Bialystok Road, there was not the least attempt that I ever heard about to organize a local militia to make a stand against the approaching invaders. In Wasilkow, there'd never ever been so much as an army recruiting station.

And then, quite suddenly, two weeks after it had begun, the War, for us, was over. Unopposed, the *Wehrmacht* occupied our town, with nary a Polish soldier, policeman, fireman, bureaucrat, or elected politician anywhere to be found. Fighting would continue elsewhere in Poland until October, but, so far as I know, no one in the entire Bialystok region fired a single shot in our defence.

———————

To say that the Jews of Wasilkow were apprehensive about their fate when the Germans set up their machine-gun and anti-tank emplacements along the Bialystok Road would be a ridiculous understatement. Even I was aware of the critical differences between the anti-Semitic generals and colonels who had succeeded Pilsudski in Warsaw and the anti-Semitic madmen who held power in Berlin. And I think we all understood that we Polish Jews could expect no better than the ravages that they had inflicted on our people in Hitler's Third Reich. What we didn't understand was the degree to which we were being optimistic.

Only my mother hadn't believed the reports coming out of Germany before the War: the Nuremberg Laws, *Kristallnacht*, the concentration camp at Buchenwald, for example, all involved concepts contrary to everything she thought and knew about the Germans. "No, no," this woman who taught me how to speak German when I was two or three years old would say, "this can't be true. It is just not possible that they would do these things. They believe in order, discipline, good manners, yes, but that is why the Germans are so scientific, so cultured and civilized. They even saved us once from a Tsarist pogrom." (Although I've never questioned the truth of this latter assertion, the where and when of it has never been clear to me.)

———

Coming back to 14 September 1939 — a Thursday: with literally nowhere to flee (we'd been caught in the jaws of the *Wehrmacht* pincers), Father thought our best bet was to keep out of sight of the Germans. Doors locked, fires out, shutters closed to the street, we made ourselves invisible. Those who did venture outside their houses on the first day of German occupation, whether Jew or gentile, were rounded up as potential spies by members of the dreaded *SS-Einsatzgruppen*, and placed under armed guard in the municipal gardens (the resting place of the disabled P.Z.L. fighter), with access to neither food nor water until they were released at nightfall.

The next day, Friday, the *SS* began gathering up the Jews who lived along the Bialystok Road. Many old men, who otherwise would have spent their day in the synagogues praying to our God to deliver His afflicted people, were put to sweeping the streets, where they were harassed and made objects of public ridicule by the *SS*. The rest — men, women, and children — were imprisoned in the Russian Orthodox church, where they were held hostage (again without food or drink, or access to sanitary facilities), under threat of death should any local resistance be encountered. Had the Nazis been there to stay, they might have burned these people alive simply to terrorize the rest of the population into submission (as they were to do to the 2,000 Jewish men they imprisoned in the Great Synagogue in Bialystok on 27 June 1941). Instead, they set them free that same evening on the petition of the White Russian priest.

On the third day, Saturday, as rumours began to circulate that they were about to leave, the German troops began looting the Jewish shops and textile mills (there were no gentile ones). Unlike

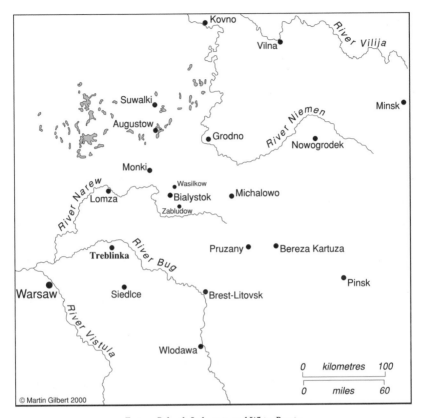

Eastern Poland, Lithuania and White Russia.

the situation in Bialystok, however, no one was murdered in Wasilkow during these daylight robberies. Until then, we'd had no notion that there existed secret terms to the German-Soviet Nonaggression Pact of 23 August 1939, which guaranteed the return of our part of Poland to Russian rule.

On the fourth day, Sunday, 17 September, the Germans began their withdrawal to positions south of the Bug River. By the next morning, there was little evidence, apart from scarred memories, that their forces had ever been in our midst.

It was on the Monday, 18 September, that my father took me to the morgue in Bialystok to show me the bodies of a dozen or so of the several hundred Jews who had been shot by the Germans during their brief occupation of the city. Apart from my baby brother, I'd never seen a dead person before, and Father apparently believed this a necessary part of my education — to toughen me up, I think. He showed me where the bullets had gone in and come out. Some of these wounds, where the blood had congealed with the earth of dusty side streets, had bits of mud sticking out of them. "See here," he said, "when we live, we're big heroes. Once we are dead, we are nothing. Just a piece of meat, and a bit of dirt." I don't know whether my father saw our future clearly then or not, but, in his own very particular way, he was preparing me to survive it by making me, at least in part, immune to some of its horrors.

I think it safe to say that if the Polish gentile majority in Wasilkow had been given their choice of armies of occupation (not that they wanted any) in September 1939, they'd have picked the Germans over the Russians. But, as *The Wasilkower Memorial Book* records, everyone in the Jewish community was in such a holiday mood on the evening of 18 September as they awaited the arrival of the Red Army that they didn't want to go to bed lest they miss any part of this historic occasion. Certainly, this is the way I remember things.

I also can confirm that everyone cheered when our neighbour from across the street, Mordechai Yurowietski, the tinsmith's son, raised a red flag on top of the fire station tower. And cheered again when a Soviet aircraft buzzed the crowd, not to rain bullets and bombs upon us, but to drop leaflets welcoming us as "Brothers and Sisters of West Byelo-Russia." And when the Soviet soldiers finally did march in the next morning, in further stark and unforgettable contrast to the Germans, they did so singing "Katiusha," with all the little Jewish and White Russian kids parading along beside them, joining in their song. This was a scene worthy of a Sigmund Romberg operetta.

What is more, once they were settled in, the Red Army servicemen, instead of stealing from us, bought everything in sight. We used to joke that when the Russians liberated us, they liberated us from butter, from sugar, from milk, from meat. Most particularly, they liberated us from western-style clothing and shoes, and everything else (from razor blades to costume jewellery), which they mailed back to their homes in Russia. We used to tell the joke about the Russian soldier who bought an alarm clock, took it to the jeweller, and said, "Just take it apart and make me a wristwatch from the pieces. The rest you can keep." I saw Russians going home in 1945 after the War with maybe a half-dozen watches on one arm. They were crazy for wristwatches.

It is true that in 1939 we experienced shortages as a result of their insatiable appetite for consumer items. It is also true that there was considerable consternation among the more religious of the Bialystok-area Jews when the Soviets imposed working conditions that violated our Sabbath, turned our shuls and synagogues into cultural centres or Red Army dormitories, and eliminated the *mikvahs* or ritual bath facilities for our women by commandeering our steambaths for their troops.

In the Mielnicki household, however, we took a positive view of the Red Army presence. For example, their takeover of our steambath, which, as I've mentioned, was only three doors up from where we lived, gave me a chance to make a few roubles. I knew from experience how hungry a person felt after he'd taken a sauna. So, whenever I could, I'd buy half a dozen large loaves of black bread, cut them into man-sized pieces, and sell these to the soldiers for a few kopecks apiece as they came out after their baths. The only drawback to their presence on our street was that when they lined up naked outside the bath, waiting for their turn to go in, they invariably would feel the need to urinate. The consequence was that within a couple of weeks the whole of Pierwszej

A typical Jewish bath house.

Brygady Street smelled of Russian piss.

And contrary to Western propaganda, being part of the Soviet Union gave the overwhelming majority of those in our communi-ty the security of belonging to a civil society, or at least one that was one hell of a lot more civil than anything we'd experienced before. I didn't know anything about the excesses of the Stalinist régime: of the millions starved to death in Ukraine in the mid-1930s, or the millions otherwise murdered or displaced, or the anti-Semitism that at least in part underlay the 1938 show trials and purges in the Russian army and civil service. What I did know was that, for the first time in my young life, I could wander the streets of Wasilkow without anyone calling me *"Jude zyd"* or "Christ killer," or throwing rocks at my head. And my sister didn't have to worry all the time about whether she was going to be raped if she missed her bus and was late coming home from work.

I even felt free to go into the Roman Catholic and Russian Orthodox churches, just to take a look. Although I found nothing particularly edifying or inspiring at the sight of a tormented, larger-than-life plaster Jesus bleeding on his cross, I thought the White Russian church, with all its intricate icons, impressively beautiful. Even my rebbe was a relatively happy man under the atheistic Communists. When the Soviets came in, he automatically received a large rouble premium — Stalin's baby bonus for people with seven or more children. There was no attempt to deny him this benefit because he taught religion — the Communist social safety net was universal in its application. When a plebiscite was held in October and November 1939 on whether we actually wanted to be part of West Byelorussia, the majority of people in the entire Bialystok area (my mother and father included) voted "Yes". And we all received Soviet passports as a result.

————

Needless to say, the wealthier Bialystoker Jews were unhappy when their mills and factories were nationalized, or their other properties confiscated and collectivized. My Uncle Eli, for example, went from being rich to being too poor to send food parcels to his son Joel, who had been captured by the Germans in the fierce fighting that had taken place around Lublin, and was now a prisoner of war in the so-called "*General Gouvernement*" area of Poland that the Nazis ruled to our south. (I should note that my cousin Joel was but one of tens of thousands of Polish Jews who fought in defence of their "homeland" — some 61,000 of the approximately 400,000 Polish prisoners of war taken by the Germans were Jews). As one might expect, my mother gladly assumed responsibility for Joel's care packages, that is, until he was sent to Germany as part of a slave-labour contingent, never to be heard of again.

Of course, Uncle Eli might have considered himself lucky that he did not share the fate of many former members of our local economic aristocracy who were sent to work camps in Siberia by the Soviets for their crimes of "speculation." It should be noted, however, that many of these political internees survived the rigours of this experience. Indeed, they would not have lived to tell their tales had they, like Uncle Eli, still been in West Byelorussia when the Germans came again in June of '41.

In Wasilkow, where the very rich did not reside, the small Jewish merchants were not so "lucky." Once their stocks were depleted, most of them were forced to close their doors and take other employment. Obviously, neither they, nor the independent Jewish craftsmen, butchers, bakers, even barbers, who were forced to form cooperatives, could have known that they had only two or three more years to live. What concerned them most when the Russians came in September 1939 was the immediate financial consequence that resulted from our integration into the Soviet system.

———————

Because our small cream cheese operation, which was all the Polish military authorities had left us, was now illegal, my father made application to the recently arrived Soviet administrator in Wasilkow, who was from Minsk, for a job in the new, state-run, cream cheese plant. It was my impression at the time that the principal reason Father became its director was because this bureaucrat felt more secure with amenable Russian-speaking subordinates than he did with inherently hostile Polish-speaking ones. The fact that Father had some relevant experience, of course made his decision possible.

Not that it could have hurt that Chaim Mielnicki was born a Russian, had a distinguished War record, had never fought with the counter-revolutionary armies, and had experienced hardship at the hands of the capitalist Poles. That he was also a Jew apparently wasn't a consideration one way or the other. In this latter connection, the story circulated in our community about the former Polish official, who demanded of this man from Minsk: "What do you intend to do about the Jews?" To which the Soviet administrator replied, "I intend to live with them, just like you are going to, if you don't want to be sent to Siberia."

Father's cream cheese factory, which was located behind the White Russian Orthodox church in the centre of town, wasn't a big operation — maybe, two, sometimes three, men, working from 5:00 a.m. until early afternoon. More importantly, it was a job that gave my father a chance to prove himself. I was astounded by the amount of raw milk (over a ton) they were able to process each day. It was almost as if the farmers in the surrounding countryside couldn't deliver it fast enough. Not that they had any choice in the matter. Under the Soviets, every aspect of the economy was state-controlled. Establishing production quotas, quality controls, and delivery schedules was obviously but the first step in the collectivization of individual farms — a prospect that could not have pleased the Polish and White Russian peasants (whose worst memories involved serfdom).

There is a long and bitter history here in terms of the relations of Poland's Jewish and peasant populations, but this is not the place for its discussion. The fact is that I don't know if the peasants who were forced to deliver their product to my father held him personally responsible for whatever fate befell them if they were reported for, say, watering their milk, or if the fact that he was a Jew served to feed their already toxic anti-Semitism. These are questions that never would have occurred to me at the time.

I loved my father's new job. For the first couple of months, until the Soviets completed their reorganization of our school system, I continued to attend classes in Wasilkow. This meant that I could go over to his little factory, which was but a five-minute walk from the school, every day during lunch hour to wash down my black bread and onion with a half-litre of fresh cream, which I drank, as I recall, from my very own zinc-coated mug.

———

I don't know exactly how my father became involved with the NKVD (the forerunner of the KGB), the Soviet intelligence and internal-security agency. Maybe the man from Minsk, or his second-in-command, the Party secretary (who was from Moscow), made this a condition of his becoming director of the cream cheese factory, but I don't think so. It couldn't have had anything to do with any of the local Communists, who had their library in our house, because the Soviets didn't trust them (the Comintern, on Stalin's orders, had dissolved the Communist party of Poland in 1938). In fact, the new administration not only packed up the library and moved it away, it sent several of the leading local Communists to Siberia (one of whom came back in 1941 — how I don't know — to serve the Nazis as a so-called "useful Jew").

Maybe Pan Wasilkowski, the resident NKVD agent, had something to do with Father's recruitment. Or maybe, having suffered a surfeit of insult and injury at the hands of the Polish fascists, he volunteered. Again, I just don't know. I do remember, however, the NKVD commissars from Moscow, who would most often arrive at our house after dark, sitting in the living room, smoking one cigarette after another until they could barely see each other through the haze, talking in low voices with Father, as they went over their lists of suspected fifth columnists (so-called *Volksdeutscher* Poles), Polish fascists, ultranationalists, and other local "traitors" and "counter-revolutionaries."

It was my understanding that he served as advisor to the NKVD about who among the local Poles was to be sent to Siberia, or otherwise dealt with. I don't think he had anything to do with the arrest of local Jews, or the expulsion of Jewish refugees who had flooded into the Bialystok area from the German-occupied provinces to the south (all of whom disappeared in the course of a single night in April 1940). Nor could he have known anything about the cold-blooded murder by the NKVD of 4,443 regular and reservist Polish officers in the Katyn Forest in April and May 1940, each of whom had his hands tied behind his back when he

Rabbi Halpern.

was shot in the back of the head, and unceremoniously dumped into one of the eight mass graves that the Nazis subsequently discovered. Certainly, it is my firm belief that no one was ever murdered at my father's behest.

Nevertheless, my mother was terribly upset by my father's collaboration with the Russian secret service. I know that this placed an additional strain on her at a time when she was already suffering from high blood pressure and had not yet recovered from whatever emotional trauma and medical complications were involved in the loss of my baby brother. I remember her begging him not to get involved. He disagreed. "We have to get rid of the fascists," he told her. "They deserve to go to Siberia. They are not good for the Jewish people."

"What about Rabbi Halpern?" she demanded. "He went to Vilna of his own accord," my father answered, "nobody was going to touch him." It had been rumoured that our chief rabbi would be put on trial by the Soviets for excommunicating one of the local Communists. Quite the opposite in fact occurred when the Soviets arrested the Party member in question and sent him to Siberia. But the strength of the rumours had panicked our rabbi into fleeing. He would spend the last two unhappy years of his life in Vilna trying to make arrangements to go to Palestine before being murdered by the Nazis in 1941.

Naturally, word of Father's clandestine activities got out. The black limousine that the commissars parked in our driveway when they came to visit was sufficient in itself to blow any cover he might have desired. Consequently, when the Germans invaded Russia in June 1941, the name of Chaim Mielnicki was on the hit lists of both the local anti-Semites (who proved more numerous than anyone imagined) and their new-found allies, the *Gestapo* (the German state secret police — part of the *SS* security structure, as opposed to its military, murder, or concentration-camp detachments). Because I was Chaim Mielnicki's son, I found myself the target of Polish bullets when I returned to Bialystok after the War. That's how much they came to hate him.

———

Historically, it was always a "Catch 22" situation for the Jews in Poland. If the Polish Christians had not treated us so badly over the eight hundred years of our existence in their midst, I doubt we would have responded so readily to any lifting of discriminatory restrictions and taxes on our collective and individual existences by our many conquerors. In the autumn of 1939, if a Polish Christian cooperated with the Russians, he might still be judged a patriot-in-waiting by his fellow Poles; if a Jew did, he was a traitor. Were we supposed to ignore what we knew was happening to the Jews in those parts of Poland which had been incorporated into the German Reich or were now part of the Nazi-ruled *General Gouvernement*, and the extent to which the Polish Christians were assisting the Germans in rounding up, robbing, terrorizing, brutalizing, and murdering our Jewish brothers and sisters? To those of us in West Byelorussia, it was obvious that the majority Polish population would never defend us.

If I can jump ahead a little bit to provide a small personal illustration of the point: in early July 1941, my father was in hiding in Bialystok. The rest of the Mielnicki family was temporarily at home in Wasilkow. We had no bread. I convinced Mother that it would be safe enough for me to join the lineup of people on the market square waiting outside Strolke Butlarz's bakery, which had been commandeered by the SS to supply the needs of the local Poles. (The Germans had been back in control since 27 June.) In that I was just another Polish kid with blond hair, and was dressed the same as everybody else, I figured I'd fit right in with the crowd. Unfortunately, one of my Polish Christian "friends" had volunteered to help the Nazi guard spot any Jews trying to buy bread. He pointed me out. A classmate of mine. I couldn't believe it.

And, in a way, I still can't believe it, although I now accept that my "friend" was merely typical of a significant percentage of Poland's Roman Catholic majority (and not the worst of them at that — he was one of those to whom I had been forced to give cookies in return for his protection at school). Of course, I don't know for certain if this kid later helped the Nazis murder Wasilkower Jews by pointing his finger to indicate who was who, or where they were hiding, but it seems likely. Certainly, many others did, when by simply doing nothing they could have saved lives that were as human and as Polish as their own. Even if the overwhelming majority of Polish gentiles didn't like Jews, or even despised us (as seems more probably the case), I will never understand how they managed to objectify us so totally. They didn't have to help the Germans destroy the Jews.

There was never any official German occupation policy that so obliged them. Yet, they gladly traded away our lives, never allowing themselves to understand that they were *Untermenschen* in the eyes of the Nazis as well. And that once all the Jews and Gypsies and Jehovah's Witnesses and homosexuals and physically and mentally handicapped people in Europe had been murdered, the Poles and the other Slavic peoples were next! Out of a population of thirty-two million Poles on the eve of the Second World War, only 5,264 (as of the end of 1999) have been honoured by the State of Israel for having helped individual Jews escape the *Holocaust* — which is only a tiny percentage of one percent of those who might have made a difference.

———

I find myself amused by the dark humour in the joke about the old Polish woman, who, during confession more than fifty years after the end of the Second World War, said to her priest: "Father, there's something that's been bothering me lately." "And what might that be, daughter?" her confessor inquired. "During the war with Germany, I hid a Jew in my cellar," she replied. "That was an entirely commendable act," said the priest. (Remember, the setting for this story is now, and the present generation of Polish priests have become enlightened, at least theoretically, about such things — especially in that there are hardly any Jews left among them to hate.) He continued: "But why are you telling me this after all these years?" The old woman hesitated for a moment, then answered, "Well, I made the Jew agree to pay me one American dollar for every day I hid him from the Nazis." The priest had to consider the weight of this disclosure for a moment — was her sin mortal or merely venial? He decided upon the latter, and granted her absolution, without penance: "That was a long time ago, daughter. If you are truly repentant, God will forgive you. Now, go in peace." "No, no," the old woman protested, "there's more: I've never told this Jew the war is over!"

———

God only knows what ghastly future Stalin, Beria, and the other Kremlin criminals had in mind for the Jews of the Bialystok region once their rule was securely established, but, so far as I was concerned, life, as it began under the Soviets, was bliss. The new administration opened a youth club. There were films, plays, and wonderful balalaika concerts to attend. Winter was nearly upon us. I was looking forward to trying out the skis I had made the previous year at school in my manual arts class. The last of the cucumbers and cabbages had been collected from the garden, and our house was filled with the pleasantly pungent odour of garlic, dill, and bay leaves. Mother was busy making great quantities of pickles and sauerkraut to see us through the months ahead. In our part of Poland vinegar was never used in pickling; instead, a small piece of black (sour rye) bread was placed in each crock of vertically quartered cucumbers to begin the fermentation process once the boiling water was poured over them to sterilize the contents, and the containers were sealed.

Whatever Mother thought about the NKVD business, Father's privileges (in addition to a decent salary) as a "comrade director" made her life easier than it would otherwise have been, especially after he was promoted to the management of another, larger cream cheese plant. The directors of the various state enterprises in the Bialystok area not only had priority access to whatever became available in the way of consumer goods, they often traded products among themselves (i.e., X kilos of cream cheese for X kilos of cottage cheese, or X kilos of carp, or X yards of fabric, or X quantity of whatever). Mother, of course, was ecstatic when Father's new-found influence created the opportunity for Aleksei to continue his education. He was able to begin engineering technology courses at a technical school in Minsk, which would enable him to work towards becoming a master weaver in one of the local textile mills. This was something that we never could have managed under a Polish régime. The quota system in secondary and post-secondary education restricted Jewish enrollment to ten percent in Polish high schools, as well as the colleges and universities. And, even had there been no war, our parents didn't have the money to send any of the Mielnicki children to school abroad, which was the practice of our richer coreligionists.

Lenka, who had graduated in 1937, was apprenticed as a pattern-joiner at what had been the Rapelski Textile Mill in Bialystok. She was very artistically inclined. In fact, she had won first prize in high school for making a beautifully detailed, pen and ink drawing of a Belgian horse, which was so highly regarded by her teachers that it was given a permanent place of honour in the school's main foyer. Of course, she went through a period of depression after she failed to gain entry to the United States in early 1939. But, at nineteen, she was already a new-age woman, and very much a part of the community of local artists.

It was at one of their cultural "happenings" a few months after the Red Army arrived that she met and fell in love with a young Russian officer called Peter (Petya) Piechka, who, as it turned out, was the son of former aristocrats. An intellectual, a Communist, an atheist: he was a good man. I liked him very much because he took an interest in what I was doing, tried to help me with some of my new Russian literature studies, and told me fascinating stories about his life in Moscow. He wasn't Jewish, but he knew a lot about Judaism because he had many Jewish friends at home, and it seems to me that he was at our house for dinner every Friday night for over a year. My parents appeared simply to accept the fact that Lenka and Peter were going to get married. If there were conversations about the implications and possible complications of a union between a Jewess and a gentile, I didn't hear them. Of course, the German invasion of Russia in 1941 brought all this to an end. Peter's regiment, along with the majority of the Red Army units in the Bialystok area, beat a hasty retreat to whatever ultimate fate, and Lenka never saw him again. She was heartbroken.

As for myself, with the tacit approval of my parents (given Father's NKVD work, it would have proved awkward for them, to say the least, had they said, "No"), once I was in high school in Bialystok, I joined the Pioneers, the Communist party youth organization for kids from ten to sixteen years of age. The Soviets provided me with everything the Polish régime had denied me. Most importantly, they welcomed me into the mainstream of their society, and gave me a red, boy-scout-type scarf, which I wore proudly round my neck to show that I *belonged*. I was taught how to march with a rifle, and fire it — activities which pleased me greatly. My membership in the Pioneers even allowed me to take an evening course in photography. The result was that, at twelve, I became an ardent supporter of the Stalinist cause. I even gave up my skiing to attend indoctrination classes. And when they showed their propaganda films, I dutifully stood up to applaud every time Josef Stalin appeared upon the screen. My one regret was that because my enriched Russian high school program involved summer school, I wasn't able to attend Pioneer camp during July and August 1940.

It never occurred to me (although it undoubtedly did to my parents) that there was any contradiction in the fact that I was at the same time studying privately in preparation for my *bar mitzvah*. Certainly, my father understood that in our new circumstances overt religious practice of any sort was not safe, and that in no circumstances did one want to bring oneself or one's family to the attention of the Soviet authorities. Consequently, my *bar mitzvah* in March 1940 was no big affair. I read a portion of the Torah in our synagogue on a Thursday morning, some candies were thrown for the children, and that was it. No party, nothing. I don't think that those few people present for the occasion were even dressed in their best clothes.

What I do remember, and have never forgotten, was our rabbi telling me that now that I was thirteen, I was a man, and responsible for my own deeds, whatever they might involve; our religion does not accept the concept that murder or other felonies committed by juveniles represent a lesser category of crime. Not even two and a half years in the death camps was enough to destroy my adherence to God's commandments. My faith in Him may have disappeared for awhile, but not my sense of right and wrong. When I was liberated from Bergen-Belsen in 1945, I could not bring myself to join my colleagues in capturing and killing our former *SS* guards. I turned away when they were being beaten to death, saying that this was a matter for God, or for the law courts. I didn't feel sorry for those Nazi bastards. I thought, "You probably deserve what's happening to you, but you should be given a chance to defend yourself in court." It was after all possible that some of them weren't even involved in the mass murder of our people.

By late 1939, Russification was the watchword of the new régime. At the Jewish high school in Bialystok, Russian replaced Polish as the principal language of instruction, and classes in Yiddish literature were discouraged. This meant that most of our instructors had to be brought from Russia. It also meant that all our new teachers were members of the Communist party. Because the Russians were strangers to Western culture, it was felt that only Party members would be strong enough to resist its corrupting influences. (This may be difficult for North American readers to appreciate, but relative to Moscow or Minsk, Bialystok was very much a Western city.) What is more, given the enormous increase in Bialystok's population as refugees (most of them Jewish) poured in following the division of Poland between Germany and Russia, our school was run on a three-shift-a-day basis in order to accommodate the influx of new students. I don't think this resulted in triple the number of instructors, but there seemed an inordinate number of them as well.

The Russian teachers were tough. Poor students were shown no mercy. They were weeded out of the academic stream by the age of twelve and sent to technical school. If they failed their vocational training, at fourteen they were put to work as apprentices in, say, the building trades or in the factories. But when the Russians saw someone capable, they pushed him to the limit, as they did with me. It's curious, given the difficulties I'd had with my Polish language classes in elementary school, that I experienced no similar problems with Russian, especially considering its employment of the Cyrillic alphabet. Because Polish uses the Latin alphabet, and Yiddish, my first language, the Hebrew alphabet, the joke would be to say that Russian was all Greek to me. However, it was not. I knew how to speak it, could read it a little, and had the advantage of a mother and father who had been educated in Russian.

What is more, as I observed earlier, Lenin's language reforms had made the New Russian far less complicated than formal Polish. Although initially, subjects like physics and algebra were made more difficult by this new language of instruction, I think my instant love of Russian literature smoothed the transition. Being introduced to the poetry of Vladimir Solovyov, and the novels of Leo Tolstoy and Fyodor Dostoyevsky proved an unexpected (and life-long) delight. Russian history, however, was a different matter. This was a very important subject to the Soviet authorities. But even I, a loyal member of the Pioneers, knew that their history had been twisted to the purposes of the Communist party. Of course, I learned it anyway, in the sense that I memorized what I needed to know to please my examiners.

I mentioned that belonging to the Pioneers gave me the opportunity to take a photography course. At school, I became the leader of our student photography club, which, in turn, led to my being chosen by my teachers for a class in motion picture production. I even secured a job in early 1941 as assistant projectionist at the Wasilkow cultural centre (formerly the largest and wealthiest of our four synagogues) for the Saturday and Sunday evening movies. My interest in taking pictures had begun a couple of years before, when my cousin Joel gave me an old box camera. It turned out that I had an eye for composition, and it wasn't long before I became the official family photographer. All the aunts were saying, "Let Mendl take the pictures. They always turn out so nice."

Anyway, I now learned how to develop photographs. And somewhere in this process, I acquired a portrait camera, which used five-by-six glass plates, from a Russian army photographer. We made an exchange, but I no longer remember what I gave him in return. (Whatever it was, it paid me back a hundred times.) I bought such darkroom equipment and supplies as I required from the money I had made selling bread to the Red Army soldiers, and from my small electrical appliance repair business. I was a born entrepreneur (another thing I didn't try to reconcile with being an ardent Communist). Then, with my parents' permission and encouragement, I set up my own studio in the apartment that had once belonged to Zutka, where Russian soldiers literally lined up on the weekend to have their photos taken so that they could send them home to their parents and sweethearts to show how good they looked in their uniforms. By the time I was fourteen years old, I had saved enough roubles to buy a motorcycle. I think perhaps that some combination of photography and film would have been my career had our world not come to a screaming halt that June.

I have nothing much to say about the German invasion of Russia on 22 June 1941 that hasn't been said a thousand times before. We were caught totally by surprise (as we had been by the German invasion of Poland in September 1939). Before the actual event, my father would have agreed with Foreign Minister Molotov's assessment: "Only a fool would attack us." I remember him saying, after the first reports of the German "Operation Barbarossa" were confirmed, "They won't get as far as Napoleon. They don't know the Russians or their winters." (In other words, the Nazis were not prepared for a winter war against millions of soldiers who wouldn't hesitate to piss on their black bread to unthaw it so that they could continue fighting when the deep snow and forty-degree-below-zero temperatures rendered German armour inoperative.) For whatever it was worth, both he and Molotov were to be proved correct — even if it took far longer to defeat the Germans than either would ever have imagined. Hitler was mad not to take the advice of his field generals, which would have resulted in the capture of Leningrad and Moscow in the summer of '41; and his failure to do so ultimately led to the turning of the tide at Stalingrad in January 1943 and the German collapse on the Eastern Front. But then, had Hitler taken other than his own counsel, Europe today probably would be ruled by his successors — a prospect too horrible to contemplate.

————

Apart from some isolated units, the Red Army did not stand to fight in our part of West Byelorussia. They retreated in total confusion. We know now that the Germans could not have cared less. Bialystok and its suburbs could be taken at their leisure, with or without a battle. When Minsk fell on 27 June, this meant that the Panzer divisions of the German Army Group Centre had enveloped the entire Bialystok salient. Surrounded, the 300,000 Russian soldiers contained therein surrendered. As in September 1939, apart from the now constant German air raids and their strafing of fleeing military and civilian traffic, those of us who lived in Wasilkow didn't know what was happening.

————

In the Mielnicki household, we were as nervous as it is possible for people to be, but we were not so terrified as to consider suicide. In Bialystok, 250 Jewish doctors, lawyers, and other professionals took the "black pill" (cyanide, I suppose) provided them by one of their number who was a pharmacist, rather than face the fate that had befallen our brothers and sisters already under German rule. I think my father's judgement was influenced by the fact that initially the Soviet officials in Wasilkow were ordered to stay put, even though they quickly lost their ability to control the town.

By the second day of the German invasion, 23 June, Polish peasants had begun robbing the Jewish stores along Bialystok Road. We again buried our valuables. My so-called Christian friends started to come by the house, saying, "Mendl, you'd better let me look after your camera [your sled, your skis, your hockey game, my whatever] until the Germans are gone. You won't have any use for it now. I'll give this back to you after the War." After the War, in August 1945, I walked down the streets in Wasilkow where these kids used to live, but they'd all disappeared.

Then, in the late afternoon of 24 June, Father's gentile friend, Emil Szymanski, who'd owned the mill at Yakimes before the Soviets took over, appeared unannounced at our door with word that the name of Chaim Mielnicki was number one on the death list of the local Polish fascists. "Chaim," he said, "you have to take your family and run. They're coming to kill you tonight." Father knew enough about Szymanski's contacts to believe him. He also knew that his friend had taken a big chance in coming to warn us. They shared a final vodka: *"L'chaim."*

After Szymanski had gone, Father told us to stop whatever we were doing and be ready to leave as soon as he got back from organizing transportation and the permits necessary to travel to the Russian interior. Mother moved the meal she was cooking to the back of the stove, and she and Lenka began to gather together such food and clothing as was practical to take with us. Aleksei took our cow next door to Mule Spektor's. And I began to dig out our wooden crate of valuables from its hiding place beneath the dirt floor of our barn. Maybe four foot by three foot by three foot — about the size of a large trunk — it was too heavy for me to lift out by myself. I had to wait for Aleksei to come back. I remember that when he did, we were in such a rush that we didn't have time to fill the hole back in. Although we did have the presence to leave the door to the garden open so that the fowl could range as they pleased.

I don't know exactly what Father had expected the NKVD would provide us when he'd hurried off to the Soviet headquarters at the town hall, but it had to have been more than the old horse and wagon with which he returned. Given the circumstances, however, none of us was about to object. We quickly bundled ourselves and our belongings onto the rotting deck of our "chariot," and set off down the road. As we did so, neighbours came out of their houses to ask: "Where are you going? How can you just leave your fine house, your wonderful garden, and everything that you own?" To complain: "Mule the Carter has his own cow; why does he need yours?" Or to protest: "The Germans are bombing the road. Like Borukh and Naftole Katz [brothers who'd lived down the street], you're going to get yourselves killed." They all thought we were mad.

It was about seven o'clock by the time we crossed the bridge over the Suprasl River, heading northeast towards Grodno. If the Wasilkow fascists had known of our departure, they could have caught up to us whenever they wanted to. The road was jammed with Russian soldiers and civilian personnel, and fleeing Bialystokers, on foot, on bicycles and motorcycles, and in all manner of vehicle. Nevertheless, we bumped along, stopping only when the scream of German Stukas sent us diving for the ditch. Three days of Nazi bombing and strafing had taken their toll. Smashed tanks, burned-out cars and trucks, dead horses and human remains littered the sides of the road. I remember the body of one man lying there with an open suitcase full of money beside him. No one made a move to touch it. And each new air attack added to this carnage.

Even worse were the cries of the wounded beseeching our help. We had no choice but to ignore them. What is more, we had to fend off those who staggered forth in their pathetic attempts to turn our open conveyance into an ambulance. All of which was profoundly upsetting to each of us, especially to Mother. Father, of course, had seen it all before. And he alone among us knew that if we stopped, or tried in any other way to help without the resources to do so, we would wind up simply adding the Mielnicki family to the body count along the road. Then, as darkness finally fell around 10:00 p.m., Red Army units, mistaking one another for the enemy, began a fusillade in the forest around us. It was frightening.

Towards first light, just after four on the morning of 25 June, Father decided that such progress as we were making wasn't worth the risk. We changed directions, and headed off along country tracks, hoping to avoid both the traffic and the Stukas. I remember we didn't talk much as we slowly zigged and zagged our way, this time heading for Zabludow, south of Bialystok, some fifty kilometres away, where, as I've mentioned, two of my mother's brothers and one of her sisters lived. In fact, Lenka, Aleksei, and I did our best to sleep until the intense heat of a Polish summer sun made this all but impossible. And although it all felt unreal, sitting there hour after hour not knowing what mortal danger might emerge from around the next bend, our journey proved without incident. As fate would have it, however, we arrived at my aunt's (the one with three sons who was married to the shoemaker) just as the *Wehrmacht* was advancing on the town.

The next morning, when some remaining Red Army artillery shelled the German line and a platoon or two of Russian infantry dug in for a fight, the Nazis responded by torching most of Zabludow, including its magnificent, 600-year-old shul, which, like the Temple in Jerusalem, had been built without the use of a single nail or piece of metal. I cannot calculate where to place this particular outrage on the seemingly endless list of German crimes. Suffice it to say that the wooden synagogue in Zabludow was one of the finest examples of what Abraham Rechtman, in his *Yidishe etnografye un folklor,* has described as "the unique creation of Polish Jewry." Before the War, architectural students came regularly from Warsaw to study it. Our shul in Wasilkow was

The schul in Zabludow.

patterned after it. Indeed, this shul was so fabulous that the Pilsudski government accorded it the status of a national historic site. In any event, the Nazis now filled it with captured Russian shells and explosives, and blasted it to kingdom come.

Of course we heard the explosion, even if we didn't know right away what it was. When we learned what the Nazis had done, my father said, "They're going to pay for this. We might not be around anymore to see it, but they're going to pay." Unfortunately, as he experienced Nazi horror after Nazi horror upon Nazi horror over the last year and a half of his life, my father would have occasion to repeat these words over and over and over again. I regret to say that so far as I can tell he was wrong in his belief in any final or divine justice. It is true that the Germans have paid something for their crimes, but they can never pay enough.

In the face of the German onslaught on the morning of 26 June, the Zabludow townsfolk fled to the nearby fields. We were no exception. Dressed in whatever we happened to be wearing, we ran for our lives, ducking and dodging, trying to keep together, with bombs exploding and bullets flying all around us. When Mother could run no further, we took cover in a ditch. Father told us to stay put, as he turned to risk his life further by retracing our steps to retrieve a couple of bundles of our clothes and bedding from my aunt's. It was while he was doing this that he encountered my three cousins, all of whom were in their late teens. They'd been separated from their parents, and each had suffered a flesh wound, either through an arm or a leg, when they were caught in the cross fire. Fortunately, contradiction though this seems, a *Wehrmacht* medic, who had set up a first aid station along an adjacent side street, had been only too glad to treat their injuries. My father now took them in tow and brought them back to where the rest of us were cowering.

When the bullets finally quit flying, we took shelter, along with several other families, in an abandoned barn. Meanwhile, the Germans advanced past us to Bialystok, which they entered on 27 June (coincidental with their capture of Minsk), and beyond to Wasilkow, Suprasl, Grodno, and all the other towns and villages in our district. While the Nazis were setting up their machine-gun and anti-tank emplacements along the nearby roads, we stayed hidden, except when scavenging for food in the cellars of Zabludow's burned-out houses. One of the remarkable things we found were quantities of new potatoes that had been baked by the heat of the smoldering timbers now collapsed around them. I still remember how delicious they tasted.

At one point, we were joined by four or five White Russian peasants who thought our presence in the barn made it an ideal place to bury the meat from their freshly slaughtered pigs. They were determined to hide it from the German army, and they reasoned that no Nazi patrol would ever think to search for more than a ton of salted and wrapped pork under the ground on which a bunch of homeless Jews were sleeping. This was a situation that might have led any Talmudic scholars in our midst to extend the definition of *tref*. Unfortunately, the question became moot when

I was spotted on one of my forays into the town by a gang of Polish peasants, who had seized the opportunity to "cleanse" Zabludow of its remaining Jewish population. I guess I gave the game away by running when one of them shouted at me. They followed me back to the barn, where they threatened to burn us out if we didn't leave. We didn't try to bargain.

My cousins now determined to go off in search of their parents. This was the last I ever saw of them. Whether they were successful or not, or whether they were murdered shortly thereafter, or later, all I know for sure is that none of them survived the *Holocaust*. Nor did their parents, or any of my other uncles, aunts, or cousins. We Mielnickis, at least, escaped Zabludow with our lives, although not with any of our possessions, save whatever we carried on our persons. I can't remember exactly how much Lenka and Aleksei had in the way of US currency, but my small collection of American dollars — my *Logschen* — were in a pouch, pinned inside my underwear. Father had Tsarist gold coins sewn into his belt, and in the false heels of his boots. And my mother had various valuables sewn into her corsets. Each of us had Russian roubles, of course, but, with the Germans now in control, cucumbers were about all I was ever able to buy with what would have been enough money to pay for a motorcycle at any time prior to 22 June.

On the road again, we heard about the mass murder of Jews in Bialystok. It was hard to believe what people told us: that the *Wehrmacht* had celebrated their arrival in the city by rounding up 2,000 Jewish males, whom they forced into the Great Synagogue before burning it to the ground; that hundreds of individual Jews had been hauled from their homes and shot in front of their wives and children; that the city's Jewish intellectuals had been trucked to a location in the direction of Wasilkow where they had been machine-gunned into a mass grave; that thousands of Jewish men and women had been forced into what amounted to slave labour (working long hours for meagre rations); that entire city blocks in

The Synagogue in Bialystok, 1922.

the Jewish section of the city had been gutted; that the German army had cordoned off the wealthier areas of what was left, and had loaded their trucks with every item of value from the Jewish homes — all of which they shipped back to the Nazi "fatherland;" that any and every Jewish protest was met with instant execution.

That all of this might be true (it was), and that the Germans at any moment might discover our existence and decide to kill us as well, involved ideas that my intellect and emotions couldn't encompass. I was just fourteen. My brother was nineteen. My sister was twenty-one. Even with what we'd already experienced, death for us didn't exist, except in the abstract. We were immortal. Our parents may have known that their lives were at an end, although I doubt this was the case on 4 July 1941, as we tried to figure out what to do next. My father knew that as long as the Russians did not abandon the War, there was hope. Stalin may have been the Devil's spawn, but he can be forgiven much for defeating Hitler.

The Białystok Synagogue after it was torched by the Germans.

The only good piece of news that we heard that day was that Wasilkow, despite its German occupation, was relatively peaceful. It was obvious that Father couldn't return to our house on Pierwszej Brygady Street, but it was possible that the rest of us might escape the wrath of the Polish fascists now that an army was back in control. We needed food and shelter, and we had both waiting for us at home — provided it hadn't been looted or occupied in our absence. The problem was how to get there. We didn't need transportation; we could walk it in six or seven hours. It was a question of getting through the German road blocks and patrols.

We decided to break up. Mother and Lenka would travel together in the daylight hours, joining the stream of refugees on the road. They would be relatively safe. At that point, the Nazis, as a rule, were only murdering Jewish males. And although rapes did happen, we thought our women more likely to be assaulted by Polish peasants than German soldiers. Aleksei and I would try to make it across country at night. Father would find his own way to Bialystok, and we hoped to the relative safety of my cousin's house (the son of one of Mother's sisters, with whom we were very close). He reasoned that the Germans couldn't kill every Jew in Bialystok, and that those Poles who had put a price on his head were less likely to find him if he were but one more poor Jew among 60,000, than if he were a prominent one among 1,500.

Amazingly, we all reached our destinations safely: hungry, tired, and dirty, but not much the worse for wear. Mother and Lenka arrived home the night of their departure from the outskirts of Zabludow. It took Aleksei and me a day longer. The only time we were in any real danger was when we heard a German patrol coming towards us as we were crossing a farmer's field. They hadn't seen us yet, and their dogs hadn't caught scent of us, but we couldn't start to run without making ourselves obvious, and there was no place to hide except for a nearby irrigation ditch. Aleksei motioned to me to follow him as he stepped into its two foot depth. When I hesitated, he whispered, "So, if they catch us we're dead," and then lay down on his back in that dirty, stinking, stagnant water, submerging everything but his nose. I did the same. I have no idea how long we actually lay there, but it seemed like hours. Finally, when the last sound of the soldiers and their dogs disappeared into the woods beyond, we dragged ourselves out.

––––––––

At home in Wasilkow, with our doors locked, fires out, and shutters closed to the street, we did our best to make ourselves invisible. We slept. We ate. Bread, as I indicated earlier, was a problem at first, but the White Russians, even some Poles, soon made it evident that they were prepared to sell, or barter for, whatever we needed. We no longer had our cow (the Germans had already confiscated all Jewish livestock), and our chickens and geese had wound up in someone else's pot, but Mother's garden was beginning to provide as much as we needed.

We were relieved when we heard that Father was safe, because the Nazis, although they publicly denied it, were suspected of having murdered the five or six thousand Jewish men they rounded up in Bialystok on 5 July — "Black Saturday," as the *Wasilkower Memorial Book* calls this particular day of infamy. The word was that the remaining 50,000 or so Bialystoker Jews were going to be crowded into an enclosed ghetto in a working class section of the city by the end of the month. Of course, we were anything but happy in Wasilkow. But apart from having to wear a yellow Star of David on our clothes whenever we went out so that our German conquerors could tell we were Jews, at least all was peaceful. That is, until late July, when the *Wehrmacht* garrison was ordered into action in Ukraine, leaving a skeleton detail of their comrades to maintain order in our town.

Apparently, this was what the Polish anti-Semites had been waiting for. The first pogrom we experienced took place the following night when gangs of local thugs began to loot individual Jewish homes. In the process, the orchestra leader, Avreml Polak, his brother-in-law, Dovid Shrabinski, the crate-maker's son, Motke Spektor, Archik the Greek, and a fine artist by the name of Shie Mongele, and twelve others, were dragged from their beds and clubbed to death in the yard of what had been the Triling Textile Factory on the other side of the Suprasl River. How do I know this? I saw their bodies.

For some reason I was out of the house the next morning — a Friday, I think — when I was caught by a pair of German soldiers in their early twenties, who were organizing a burial party for the pogrom victims (which was the extent of any official investigation into the deaths of these unfortunate men). I forget now whether I was given a shovel or was told to bring one. In any event, I never did get to use it. One of the people conscripted to our group was Walper Kowalski, the Jewish community's much respected *shochet* (ritual slaughterman). When the Germans found out who he was, they told him to fetch his prayer shawl and Holy Book. At the Triling yard, they ordered the rest of us to lie face down on the pavement, while they and a couple of their comrades had a little "sport" with Mr. Kowalski. They began by hacking off his side-curls and beard with their knives. When he didn't react as they expected, they started to smash him with their fists and rifle butts. They knocked him to his knees. Then they picked up a couple of our shovels and started to hit him across the back. And the more they beat him, the more excited these young Nazis became. We were ordered not to look. Mr. Kowalski uttered not a word. Nor did he when they soaked his shawl in gasoline and made him put it around his shoulders. Had he begged for his life maybe they wouldn't have lit it on fire, but he didn't, and they did. Perhaps to their dismay, he didn't scream. The words he finally spoke were in prayer. I heard the burning gas. I saw the flame. I smelled the *shochet's* burning flesh. Then I fainted.

When I regained consciousness, they were dropping the corpses, including Mr. Kowalski's, into a common grave. The soldiers joked that they had been just about to bury me as well. I stumbled home. I couldn't stop shaking. I said to my mother, "They burned the *shochet*. I can't believe they did this. They burned the *shochet*." This I always remember as one of my first most-horrible times. I was haunted by that smell of burning flesh. I did not yet know that I was going to a crematorium where I would smell it all the time, day and night.

The cold-blooded murder of our *shochet* by the Germans was understood by the local gentiles as a sign that they'd been given *carte blanche* to pillage and murder among us as they pleased. Two days later, on Sunday, they came out of their church after mass led by a young priest who screamed, "Death to the Christ killers!" Their object: to rob us of all our possessions, then drown the entire Wasilkow Jewish community in the Suprasl River. An older Catholic cleric tried to restrain them. "Don't harm our Jewish brothers," he protested. The mob ignored him. They picked up their clubs, studded with nails, bolts, and metal springs, picked up their sickles, their scythes, their chains, their two-by-fours, and began to march from their end of town towards ours, chanting, "No more Jews in Wasilkow." Their "New Era" had arrived.

I forget where Aleksei was that day — probably visiting one of his gentile girlfriends in Bialystok. However, when Mother and Lenka heard these psychopaths coming down our street, they took shelter next door, hoping, I think, that there might be safety in numbers. Afraid to leave the only sanctuary I had ever known, I refused to go with them. Instead, I hid among the empty boxes and barrels in the attic. That is, until I heard the screams of a woman in the street. I crept to the window and looked out to witness one of our very pregnant neighbours being beaten to death with clubs and two-by-fours. When moments later these assassins left her to shatter our front door, I opened the window and leapt out.

Too terrified even to consider that I might have broken my leg on the cobblestones below, I ran to find my mother. I was convinced that if they found me, these so-called Christians would either beat me to death, or torture and set me on fire, as the Germans had our *shochet*. I had just managed to squeeze under a couch in the corner of our neighbour's front room when half a dozen of these racist crazies burst in, swinging their clubs at everyone in sight, including our neighbour's elderly father, and my mother, who was black and blue for weeks thereafter. In attempting to ward off one of these maniacs, Lenka had the skin sliced from the back of her hands by his razor-sharp sickle. There was blood all over the place. Had I known how, which I didn't, I couldn't have helped my mother or my sister. I couldn't move. I could barely breathe.

Once these criminals had driven everyone, except me, into the street, they began to loot and vandalize the house: pulling out drawers and emptying cupboards in their search for money, gold, and other hidden treasures; carting out the silver salvers and candelabra, and whatever took their fancy; then destroying everything else. Windows, pictures, mirrors, and dishes were smashed. Pillows, quilts and mattresses were ripped apart until the house was filled with down and feathers. "Don't damage. Don't damage. It's all ours," one of these bandits yelled, trying to stop them. Which prompted some of his companions to haul out their cocks to piss on what they hadn't yet been able to demolish.

The sheer ferocity of the attack on our community appears to have frightened even the German soldiers, and a few of the older reservist-types tried to restore order by firing their rifles into the air. When this failed to have any effect on the mob, they phoned *Wehrmacht* headquarters in Bialystok for help. Reinforcements arrived just in time to prevent these Polish barbarians from forcing a crowd of Jews off the bridge over the Suprasl. I wasn't there to see this, but the *Wasilkower Memorial Book* records that when the officer in charge learned what these blood-crazed animals were about to do, he shouted, "Polish swine! Get out of here right now."

In retrospect, however, it would seem obvious that this was no Nazi angel of mercy come to rescue Jews from a watery grave (although I am certain that every Jew present experienced a sense of overwhelming relief, maybe even gratitude, at being saved). Wasilkow's Polish fanatics had challenged German authority. In no circumstances could this be tolerated. The *Wehrmacht* officer was there to put these other *Untermenschen* in their place. Otherwise, I doubt he cared one hoot about their robbery and murder of Jews.

When I finally managed to crawl out from my hiding place, there was no sign of life in any of the neighbourhood houses, including our own. Pierwszej Brygady Street was deserted, except for the dead. Fortunately, I suppose, they numbered no more than twenty or twenty-five, and most of the houses showed little signs of serious damage. I found those of our people whom the Germans had *saved* — "bedraggled, wounded, and in a miserable state," as I wrote in my 1945 deposition on this event — outside the German command post, where an *SS* cinematographer was setting his motion picture camera on a heavy wooden tripod so that he could record for propaganda purposes how the *civilized* Germans stopped the *barbaric* Poles from killing the *pathetic* Jews in their midst!

It was at this point that Mother decided that we would leave Wasilkow forever. We salvaged such as we could from the wreckage of our home, which wasn't much. I never thought of this at the time, but these fascist robbers must have been sorely disappointed as they sorted through Chaim and Esther Mielnicki's earthly possessions. The wooden crate containing all our valuables had been abandoned in Zabludow. I did take note, however, that my father's prized painting of Adam and Eve in the Garden of Eden was not among the broken bits and pieces strewn about the living room floor. That very night we slipped away to join Father in the Bialystok ghetto.

I should add that fifteen months later there were "No more Jews in Wasilkow." Indeed, it was officially decreed *"Juden frei"* (free of Jews). Our houses, most of them in prime condition — fully furnished, food in the cupboards and cellars, clothes that maybe even fit hanging in the closets — were given *free* to Polish peasants from the countryside. The Nazis had "saved" the Wasilkower Jews from the Poles in order to send every last one of them to the Treblinka death camp. And to make prophetic the words, "Don't damage. Don't damage. It's all ours."

In the Bialystok ghetto, the five of us were quartered in one of the two bedrooms in an apartment on Fabryczna Street, in what had been a working-class area of the city. Another family occupied the smaller second bedroom, and a third was assigned the unpartitioned living-room space through which the rest of us had to pass whenever we opened our doors. The tiny kitchen, in which there was barely enough room for the three mothers to stand at the same

Wasilkow Jewish properties without Jews.

time, was communal, as was the highly odoriferous toilet for which twelve or fourteen people had to compete. The only good thing was that nobody had babies to keep everyone awake at night. (The original gentile occupants of this slum-dwelling had been moved gratis to an upscale, formerly Jewish, apartment building.) Initially, we had no furniture, except for two beds. Mother and Lenka slept in one; Father and I in the other. Aleksei slept on a straw-filled pallet on the bare wooden floor. Then Father managed to purchase a wooden packing case, which he placed between the two beds so that it might serve both as a secure (he'd also organized a hasp and padlock) storage for our food and as a table on which to eat it. Thus did we fill to capacity our sixteen- or seventeen-foot-by-twenty-foot space, which, I might add, was commodious by ghetto standards.

On the positive side, the ghetto was self-contained, in the sense that it was exclusively Jewish, and that inside its walls, at least we didn't come in contact with any Polish or Nazi fanatics. We were in hiding. Whether there was an actual price on my father's head I don't know, but we'd been informed that there were men from Wasilkow keeping an eye on each of the ghetto's three gates hoping for a glimpse of him. We thought they might be patrolling our compound's perimeter as well. And because we were on the ground floor, with a window facing the wooden fence that marked our "sanctuary's" boundaries, we kept a blanket over it. We took comfort in the thought that if no one could see us, nobody could touch us. As long as we had food, we felt secure. It was no doubt just as well that it never crossed our minds that any day they chose to the Nazis could come in (as they did in 1943) and pack up the whole ghetto and send it all the way to the ramps of Treblinka.

Certainly we were luckier than a lot of people. As I noted earlier, over fifty thousand Jews had been crammed into the Bialystok ghetto. Wall to wall. We were practically walking on top of each other. People were sleeping in the streets because there simply wasn't enough accommodation. Our advantage was that Father's cousin, Pejsach Melnicki, was one of the twenty-four Jews appointed to the *Judenrat* (Jewish council) that administered the ghetto (under rules and conditions imposed by the Nazis, of course). I suspect that Pejsach did not approve of my father's Russian ways, which is the only explanation I can offer for the fact that none of the rest of us had met, or were ever to meet him. Nevertheless, blood proved thicker than water, and, unlike many others, we had a roof over our heads from the first day. Our cousin was also able to make sure that there was never any official record of our presence. This meant that the Polish fascists couldn't track us down. And neither could the *Gestapo* when they took up the search. We didn't exist.

We also had the advantage of having quite a bit of American money. Amazing stuff, Yankee currency — for one United States dollar we could buy seven kilos of black-market bread, or several kilos of potatoes or, when we could find some peasant who had it for sale, several litres of skim milk. This kept us alive, if not exactly fit. The only person whose health seemed to improve on a regimen of 200 grams of black bread and a couple of boiled potatoes a day was Mother — in the sense that she lost much of her excess weight, which appeared to help her high blood pressure. I guess all our stomachs had begun to shrink, which should have made our limited rations more acceptable. However, I was hungry all the time, as well as being bored silly by the monotony of our diet. Lenka and Aleksei must have felt the same way, because I remember the excitement we shared when I once found a jar of mustard in the corner of an otherwise empty top shelf in the kitchen. We were eating boiled potatoes with just the tiniest bit of mustard spread over their skins as if they were a delicacy.

Of course, there were many people poorer than we were in the Bialystok ghetto. Everywhere you turned there were beggars. The ones you really had to feel sorry for were those who, for the first time, were completely dependent on the charity of their relatives or on the totally inadequate resources of the *Judenrat*. Elderly parents and young mothers with broods of children whose respective sons and husbands had been murdered by the Nazis often lacked even the most rudimentary survival skills. As did many of the upper and middle class people who somehow had managed to keep their personal wealth intact under the Soviets. Now robbed by these German barbarians of everything they owned or had ever cherished, including their established places in society, they were unable to adapt to ghetto life. Then there were those whose minds had been unhinged by their experiences in that first month of Nazi rule. In the normal circumstances of *shtetl* or ghetto life, the women of the community organized such charity as was necessary and reasonable to look after those who had neither the means nor

Jews of Bialystok move into the ghetto.

the mental competence to tend to their daily needs. I remember
my mother always trying to help one family in Wasilkow who didn't
have the brains between them to cart out their buckets of pee,
never mind do anything else. In the ghetto, this was not possible.
You cannot share what you do not have.

Simply put: if you were unable to fend for yourself, or didn't
have anyone to fend for you, you would not get enough to eat. In
a place where sanitary conditions were minimal and diseases like
typhoid fever rampant, if you became malnourished, as so many
did eating only the few potatoes or the watery soup the *Judenrat*
could provide, you weren't destined to live long. There wasn't a day
when scores of foul-smelling corpses weren't collected for burial,
including the bodies of those people who, in their desperation,
had committed suicide in the night, and those of newborn babies,
whose little lives had been snuffed out by mothers unable to feed
them. The ghetto had its own cemetery behind Katok's mill on
Polna Street, but in these circumstances, its operation was anything but in conformity with Jewish burial law.

For those men and women in the ghetto who were able and willing, it is true that there were "jobs" to be had. The Nazis had taken over the Bialystok factories, and demanded what amounted to Jewish slave labour to run them. Wages were paid in food rations that were barely enough to keep body and soul together. The German military also required that the ghetto provide its daily quota of thousands of labourers for road work, demolition, construction, domestic service — whatever. If there were not enough volunteers for whatever the Germans required, the *Judenrat* police, the so-called "Jewish Law Enforcement Service," armed with night sticks or rubber truncheons, would round up any shortfall. Finally, the *Judenrat* itself employed people in various capacities, thus allowing them to earn a bit of bread.

Aleksei and I were keen to work, but only inside the ghetto, where we would be safe. Father couldn't take the chance of doing anything that would draw attention to his existence. Indeed, he seldom left the shadows of our locked room in the daylight hours, unless it was to buy our weekly supply of bread. And this he did at seven a.m., each Monday. Mother was in a position similar to Father's. And Lenka was suffering from an incapacitating depression. Thus did the Mielnicki boys assume the position of family bread-winners. We would report to the Jewish community centre first thing, six mornings a week. If we were lucky, we would be put to work doing minor building repairs or sweeping the streets. At the end of the day, the *Judenrat* would pay you one quarter of a loaf of bread, 250 grams. It wasn't much, but anything that added to our family's rations was welcome.

In the evenings, there were educational classes, poetry readings, plays even, for those who wanted to attend. I didn't. Maybe because I had yet to recover from my recent experiences in Wasilkow, maybe something else, I don't know, but I was reluctant to venture forth at night. I preferred to sit around and talk with the new friends I had made on the street where we now lived. Hopes. Dreams. Politics. God. How, if any of us survived, we would change the world. With or without God. We were very much upset with God. If we were his Chosen People, did He know what He was doing? Personally, I gave up on Him. I don't feel that way today, but neither do I quarrel with how I felt when I was fourteen years old.

At nineteen, Aleksei was more concerned with having a good time than he was with issues of divine providence. When darkness fell and the curfew went into effect, he'd dodge the *Judenrat* police on one side of the ghetto fence, and then the patrols of the *SS-Einsatzgruppen* and the Polish police on the other, to go visit his girlfriends. Young, handsome, full of fun, with a beautiful tenor voice, he was a charmer. Apparently, the gentile women of his age (and undoubtedly the older ones as well) lost all control when he sang "Catherinette," or any of the other hits of that French heart-throb, Tino Rossi. That Aleksei never got caught on his romantic adventures into Bialystok indicates that we could have escaped the ghetto had we wanted to. It wasn't the wall or the fence, or the threat of beatings by the *Judenrat* police or being thrown in the ghetto jail, or being shot dead by the Polish or the *SS* patrols that kept us inside. It was the fact that, surrounded by enemies, once out, we had no place to go. This didn't mean that we didn't consider this question very seriously. We did. But before I go into the particulars of the Mielnicki family's deliberations here, there is one more of Aleksei's experiences I think important to relate.

One morning in September, when he was in the wrong place at the wrong time, that is to say near the main ghetto gate at Jurowiecka and Sienkiewicza Streets, where a large *SS* work gang (or *Kommando*) was being assembled, he was grabbed by a *Judenrat* policeman and consigned to its ranks. Consequently, he was one of maybe two hundred or more Jews transported by truck to a ravine several kilometres outside Bialystok that the Soviets had used as a military storage depot for tanks and artillery. As I understand the story, this site had been turned into a mass grave for several thousand bodies, and their task that day, and every day for the next two weeks, was to move earth over these rotting corpses. According to what Aleksei later told Father and me, although the bodies had been decomposing throughout the summer under a thin covering of lime, it was obvious that they had to be the remains of the Black Saturday martyrs, many of whom had been relatives, friends, or neighbours of those now obliged, *under threat of death*, to shovel dirt over what was left of them.

At the time, I could only imagine their shock, their horror, their indignation, combined, as it had to be, with a violent physical reaction to the overpowering stench of that still rotting flesh. At fourteen, I thought I'd seen and smelled my share of dead bodies, including those of people I knew and liked, but five or six thousand? It was quite beyond me. Of course, it went without saying that their *SS* guards were perverts, and I wasn't surprised at Aleksei's account of the pleasure they took in ordering the ghetto inmates to begin: "*Schnell, schnell,* you Jewish swine, get to work!" I could also understand that it would have been folly for anyone to have refused, unless he wanted to add his body to those already in the pit.

The *SS*, with their death's-head badges on their caps, were a nasty lot at the best of times. Drunk, they were out of control. And these ones either were issued rations of vodka, or were allowed to bring their own to help them contend with this "unpleasant" assignment. Leaning against their vehicles, which were parked as far back from the stink as they could get and still keep guard, by noon they would be singing barracks' ballads. Once, when the ground where Aleksei was standing gave way and he began to slide into the pit, one of them yelled, "Leave him." His comrades obviously thought him a great wit and laughed uproariously when he offered a toast to "One more dead Jew." Two of my brother's companions undoubtedly risked their lives to pull him out. At the end of their twelve-hour shift, the work party was returned to the ghetto gate, where each member was paid a half bread (500 grams). Our mother was pleased with the extra ration. Aleksei, of course, never told her how he'd earned it. Our father said, "They're going to pay for this. We might not be around anymore to see it, but they're going to pay."

It was a week or two later that the *Gestapo* presented a list of Jews they wanted to "interview" to the *Judenrat*. Father's name was on it. As usual, the *Judenrat* had forty-eight hours to carry out this order, or the ghetto would suffer severe sanctions. When we heard about this, we were scared to hell. We wanted to get out of Bialystok as fast as possible, because we knew that there was a high probability that the *Judenrat* would decide that the collective interest of 50,000 people demanded that they give my father up. In which case, the Nazis would torture and kill him. Coincidental with this order, however, was a separate *SS* command that 6,000 Jews be ready the next morning for transport to the town of Pruzany, in a forested region a hundred and fifty or so kilometres to the southeast.

"Pruzany?" people in the ghetto asked. "What's at Pruzany? Nothing. Some poor peasant farms, logging camps, and a few sawmills. For what do they need 6,000 more Jews at Pruzany?" There was wide belief that these 6,000 would be machine-gunned into some nearby ravine, just like the Black Saturday martyrs. Nevertheless, we agreed to let Father's cousin arrange for us to be included anonymously in that transportation. Lenka was really in no condition to make an independent decision, but Aleksei and I were given our choice of options: 1) we could stay behind, possibly keeping Lenka with us, in what we all thought was the relative safety of the Bialystok ghetto; 2) Aleksei and I could escape the ghetto to join the Russian partisans who were rumoured to be fighting behind German lines (that is, if we could find them, and if they would accept us); or 3) we could risk death by going with our parents. For us there was no choice. There never would be. The Mielnickis were a family.

The *Bialystoker Memorial Book* states that the 6,000 Jews sent to Pruzany were "savagely tortured." If they were, I never witnessed any of this, and we lived there for over fourteen months. People were occasionally shot, and no doubt there were many individual cases of abuse, but compared to Bialystok, Pruzany was an improvement. And from what my brother told me about his experiences doing forced labour in one of the nearby logging operations, no one was tortured there either. It is true that conditions in these bush camps were primitive: lice, poor food, inadequate clothing, and long hours working in sub-zero temperatures. It is also true that there were people that either froze to death or were murdered if caught trying to escape. But that was it. Nothing out of the ordinary — relatively speaking of course. When the Germans closed the camp during the spring breakup in 1942, Aleksei and the other young men who'd been conscripted to work the winter there were sent "home."

The only grisly story that I recall from our Pruzany days happened one morning in December 1941, just before Aleksei was assigned to felling trees. The *Judenrat* police banged on our door and ordered my brother out of the house to help dig a grave for a partisan who'd been shot by a German patrol the previous night as he tried to enter the ghetto. Aleksei later told me that, try as they might in the time allotted for this task, his work party couldn't make more than a fairly small, maybe a metre in diameter by half-metre deep hole in the frozen ground. And that in the end they'd been forced to cut this Jew into pieces in order to bury him. Nothing was sacred anymore, but there was no "savage torture."

Without fear of contradiction, I, however, can state that had Aleksei and I chosen to remain in Bialystok, I would not be alive today. Our move to Pruzany is one of many events that ultimately saved my life. Indeed, we had the feeling that everything was going to be all right when we were loaded *in orderly fashion* onto large, tarpaulin-covered, *Wehrmacht* troop transports, with *Wehrmacht* drivers. Despite our individual and collective experiences with earlier German army atrocities, we knew that the *Wehrmacht* didn't generally perform death-squad functions. In any event, the trucks proceeded at what seemed a pretty easy-going pace, and we arrived at our destination towards evening.

I don't know who Father had had to *schmear*, or how much money was involved, but we were immediately allocated our own two-bedroom house. Maybe he parted with one of his gold coins. Normally, he wouldn't have considered doing such a thing. Whenever the subject came up (which was not often), he would say, "These are not for spending. They're for starting a new business when Hitler is defeated." Possibly he'd made an exception in order to buoy Mother's sinking spirits. Although she looked healthy enough, she was no longer convinced that she could or would survive. In fact, I don't think she thought that any of us would emerge from our situation alive. You could see the worry always on her face. And it was the thought of her children dying before any of them had really had a life that ground her down a little every day.

The problem was that there was never any good news while we were at Pruzany. A couple of people in the ghetto had made their own radios, despite this being a *capital* offence under the rules laid down by the Germans. Of course, everyone was anxious to have any news that could be picked up from the British and Russian shortwave stations. This was a mistake. Leningrad had been under siege since early September. The *Wehrmacht* had pushed through Ukraine, where the Russians lost a million men, into Crimea. And until they were stopped by an early and brutal winter, it looked as if the Germans might take Moscow. Russia was on its knees, and it seemed as though all Europe would soon be enslaved by the Third Reich. We didn't need to hear about this. Nor did we need to know about the Japanese victories at Pearl Harbor, Hong Kong, Singapore, Manila, and Rangoon. Our last best hope, Britain and the United States, had been dealt a critical blow, or so it seemed to us. Then, we started to get word from the partisans, who were operating in the forest around us, about the mass murder of hundreds of thousands of Jews throughout Poland, the Ukraine, and Russia. They told us about the gas chamber at Chelmno and the burning of thousands of Jewish bodies on gigantic pyres, and about the other concentration camps at Treblinka, Sobibor, Majdanek, Belzec, and Auschwitz-Birkenau. This put us all into a state of despair. We were engulfed by a sense of helplessness as we contemplated the end of our lives.

There was no ghetto *per se* at Pruzany, in the sense of our being confined by a wall or a fence. Initially, at least, the Germans had something else in mind for us. Our purpose was to displace the hundreds of White Russian families in a section of the town bordering the forest, who'd been a source of supply for the Russian partisans who were operating in the area. Thousands of slowly starving Jews living in squalor, the Nazis calculated, could provide succour to no one. Practically every family was doubled up or tripled up in terms of sharing accommodation, either in the newly vacated White Russian houses or in those of the relatively small (maybe 2,000) resident Jewish population. What the Germans apparently hadn't taken into account was that we might become a source of recruits for the small band of Jewish partisans, who were also organizing nearby. We were spread out to such a degree that the military had difficulty maintaining effective perimeter patrols. Consequently, anyone who wanted to could wander off into the surrounding forest at night, never to be seen again. That they were most likely to die out there was another consideration.

As I said earlier, the house into which we moved had two bedrooms. Mother and Father slept in one, Aleksei and I in the other. Lenka slept in the small front room. The beds, I might mention, were made of planks, with straw-filled mattresses. Because the straw broke down quickly, you were in effect sleeping on a solid surface — which is no great problem if you're tired enough, and if you're warm. Our new home's only source of heat, the kitchenette's wood-burning stove, however, did present a problem: firewood — there wasn't any. And we weren't allowed to cut down trees. Winter (freezing rains and snow) set in as we arrived, with the consequence that Aleksei and I spent some part of every night stealing boards from neighbourhood fences so that we could cook and keep out the cold. We shared a well (which we insulated against the freezing temperatures with piles of straw). The outdoor privy was at the back of the property, maybe fifty metres from the house.

Still, after Bialystok, we were happy to have a space to call our own, enough water to keep us clean, and a toilet we didn't have to share. And for a while, our diet actually improved. There were still potatoes, radishes, and onions in our house's snow-covered back garden. They were sometimes half-rotten, but, washed and cooked, they were edible, and delicious I thought. The only time I remember eating meat in Pruzany was once when I was able to trade a pair of gold earrings that I'd found while repairing a porch for a half-kilo of bacon. To our mother's disgust, Aleksei and I cut this into tiny cubes and fried them in a pan with a couple of onions and our ration of potatoes. It was terrific. But there was a price to pay, as there was every time you didn't restrain yourself, when, on those rare occasions, there was more than enough to eat. God forbid if somebody was abusing food. He got diarrhoea.

Father, of course, had no idea as to whether the *Gestapo* would pick up his trail and follow him to Pruzany. He was pretty nervous those first couple of weeks, and inclined to spend most of his time at home with Mother, fixing things around the house. I thought he was afraid of his own shadow. But when no men in black leather coats and fedoras arrived to take him away, he settled down. Although still inclined to look over his shoulder a lot, he began to take occasional *Judenrat* jobs within the ghetto, thus earning some potatoes, carrots, or bread for his efforts. When suitable work was not available, he had our cache of American dollars to fall back on. In addition, when he found a large, Russian leather map case in our attic (material much in demand for soling boots and shoes), he was able to barter pieces of it for beans and barley and things when the White Russian farmers came to sell their produce each Thursday. Ghetto life, even at Pruzany, was hard on my father. Although he did his best to keep up a brave front, he felt useless. The one thing that he couldn't hide from us was his hair, which turned from jet-black to solid grey.

Aleksei and I remained our family's principal breadwinners at Pruzany. The *Judenrat* provided each *family* with 250 grams of bread a day, which wasn't enough to stay alive on. The rest you had to earn, and we always had jobs of some sort. Mother spent most of her day cooking, cleaning, washing, and sewing patches upon the patches on our clothes. Not even the black market provided access to new boots or clothing, so that whatever wore out, wore out. By the time we left Pruzany in December 1942, we all looked like ragamuffins — which served further to destroy our self-esteem, and thus weaken by another degree or two our ability to resist the Nazi death machine.

That first winter, I worked ten hours a day, most days, at the home of Pruzany's Mayor or Burgermeister (really a Nazi Party appointee), sawing, splitting, and piling firewood in the freezing cold in return for my quarter kilo of black bread. I remember that I had to keep stopping to rub my hands together because my gloves had lost most of their fingers. I don't think this Nazi colonel ever acknowledged my presence (he wasn't *SS- Einsatzgruppe* — he wore a uniform that I remember as being yellow in colour; of the sort that Hermann Göring wore). His wife, however, at least seemed concerned that I might freeze to death in her yard. After her husband returned to work in his chauffeur-driven limousine following his mid-day meal, this kind woman would bring me out a plate containing the remains of their soup, which was often thick with vegetables. After Aleksei came back from the bush camp in the spring of 1942, and my job cutting wood every day for the Mayor had come to an end, I tried always to make certain that I was assigned to the same labour *Kommando* as my brother. I was scared silly that if I were sent out on an individual assignment, I might not be as lucky as I had been at the Mayor's, and would wind up working for some Nazi who would beat and abuse me.

All things considered though (and relatively speaking of course), Pruzany was a good ghetto. And this remained so, even after we lost our house at the beginning of 1942. Probably in response to partisan sabotage in the area (and undoubtedly to rumours that ghetto inmates were escaping into the woods), the German command decided to consolidate the living area assigned to its prisoners. Our house was just outside the new ghetto perimeter. Consequently, the five of us were consigned to a room in one of the original Pruzany Jewish homes. Our arrival made for three families (twelve people) sharing a simple, peasant-type cottage. The only compensation was that our host-family was generous and kind. I can picture them — the father had difficulty walking because he had had a stroke — but I can't recall their names. What I do remember is that our diet there was mainly black bread and watery soup. Fortunately, I suppose, my stomach had shrunk even further, so that, while still possessed of a gnawing hunger that never went away, I couldn't eat very much anyway.

What worried me more at the time was that Mother began to get thinner than the rest of us. However, it is only in retrospect that I realize that in order to make certain that her children had enough nourishment to sustain them, she was not taking her share. When Aleksei and I worked in the Pruzany cream cheese factory during the summer of '42, I once managed to smuggle a couple of litres of skim milk and a few hundred grams of butter past the guards at the ghetto gate as a special treat for her. She didn't want it. She used the milk to make pellet-like biscuits from some bran my father had acquired, and insisted that the rest of us eat the butter with our bread. This was the only time we ever argued.

As in Bialystok, a *Judenrat* ran the ghetto, as per instructions from Pruzany's Burgermeister. Apart from patrolling the boundaries of our compound, however, the regular German military weren't that much in evidence. They used the Polish police to control the ghetto entrance, which was fortunate, because a lot of our gentile compatriots were bribable. For a bottle of vodka (which was a standard medium of exchange), if they knew no German was watching (if caught, they'd be shot), they would turn a blind eye to an extra load of carrots or potatoes being delivered to the Jewish community centre. Of course, the Burgermeister himself, whose ambition was personal enrichment, might demand that the *Judenrat* collect three kilos of gold, five kilos of gold, or the equivalent in thousands of dollars from the ghetto inmates. Right away. Forty-eight hours. His "price" for fighting off *SS* demands, real or invented, that the ghetto be immediately liquidated. This was the norm for Burgermeisters in Nazi-occupied Europe. It was the German Mayor who didn't try to blackmail us out of our last dollar who was dangerous. A *pure* Nazi. A killer. Someone who would never argue that he needed his Jews because they were producing for the German war machine, etc. — thus postponing our transport to Auschwitz, and so paying for his retirement estate in Bavaria in the process. *Pure* Nazis were racial fanatics, who couldn't have cared less about stuffing their pockets at our expense. They were content to have the *SS* rob us of everything we had, including our hair and the gold in our teeth, once we arrived at their death camps. And the sooner they got us there, the better.

There was a rabbi and a *shochet* in the ghetto at Pruzany, but I don't know how they managed to support themselves. Maybe as learned men they taught in the primary school that the *Judenrat* had set up to teach the young kids how to read and write. Certainly I never remember being in touch with these people. Or going to any synagogue. My father may have gone, but not I. Not my brother. We had other things to do on the weekends when we were free. We had sleep to catch up on, friends to visit, games to play, and meetings to attend. And when we weren't free, we did these things at night. There was the same ten-o'clock curfew as there had been in Bialystok, but we had ways of getting back and

forth without the *Judenrat* police who enforced it finding out. Five
or six of us regularly played dominoes or cards, often until one or
two in the morning. (I'd cut fifty-two cards out of some old shoe
boxes, and appropriately embellished them with hand-drawn
kings, queens, knaves, and appropriate suits — they were a little
heavy, but no one complained.) Five or six hours later, seven days
a week, Aleksei and I had to report to the Jewish community
centre for work, but there were days when they didn't need us.
Alternatively, we would attend Communist party meetings at
night. Although this was where we first met the Jewish partisans,
mainly we listened to our older Party comrades talk about how we
were going to restructure things after the War. The Bundists and
the Zionists had their own organizations in the ghetto as well, so
there was something for every ideological bent.

I don't recall Aleksei having any serious romantic adventures
in Pruzany, although he may have. At twenty years old, he was at
his sexual prime. And human. I had my fifteenth birthday there
on 20 March 1942, and, however malnourished, was not immune
to hormonal urges. There were young women our own ages in the
ghetto, who were possessed of the same natural desires. I know I
was friendly with a couple, but apart from some occasional kissing
and groping in the dark, we held ourselves in check. This wasn't
so much a question of morality as it was an overwhelming fear of
pregnancy on the part of the girls. I didn't argue. I'd seen enough
dead babies in the garbage. I was mature enough to understand
that sex was intended to create life, not kill it. It is perhaps interesting to note that however bad the conditions at Pruzany, women
still menstruated, whereas in the full horror of the death camps, it
is reported that their periods stopped entirely.

Pruzany, as I've mentioned, was on the edge of a great forest:
the Puszcza Bialowieska (which today is a national park, and home
to some of the few remaining European bison). This was ideal
country for partisans, and the Russians, Poles and Jews all were
active in the area. Indeed, many of our ghetto colleagues heeded

the call of the Jewish partisans: "Save your lives and join us." Aleksei and I talked to our parents about this. I remember Mother saying, "For us, it's too late. We are too old." She was thirty-nine. "We've had our lives, but we want you to survive. You have to save yourselves." Father agreed. They were pushing us to go. Mother said it was our duty to survive if we could. Lenka was not part of this discussion. Living like a rabbit in a hole in the ground, for her was not an option.

We talked about all this, my brother and I. In many ways, we were tempted to go, if only to break the monotony of our existence. Fourteen months in the Pruzany ghetto was like an eternity. Almost every day was grey. We were surrounded by misery. The 6,000 Jews who had been transported from Bialystok to Pruzany were from among those least able to fend for themselves. The *Judenrat* did its best for them, but the majority were already at the end of their lives, even if they didn't know it. They'd been systematically terrorized, starved, overworked, and degraded: stripped of whatever sense of personal worth they'd ever had. And death continued to surround us, even if its causes were now mainly diseases in bodies so weakened by hunger that they could not resist the slightest infection.

How many times had Aleksei and I asked ourselves: "Are we then like everyone else here, content to do nothing but exist, while we wait for the end of our lives?" As we saw things, we weren't much different from wild animals struggling every day just to get enough food to stay alive. We wondered: "Why are other people free, when we are not? How much worse could it be with the partisans?" Then we said, "How can we leave the parents alone when they need us so much? We don't do that in a Jewish family. Whatever happens to the family happens to you. You stick together." We told our father and our mother: "We've made up our minds. We won't go. We feel the same as we did when we talked about this in Bialystok. If we have to die, we'll die together. If we live, we'll survive together." Noble sentiments to be certain, but ones that quickly proved naive in the extreme.

We had presumed, even in our captivity, a certain control over our individual destinies. In the event, we had none. As a family, we would be torn asunder within months by the Nazis, some to die, some to live, none to stay together. I should note, however, that virtually all of our colleagues who did join the partisans were killed before the War's end. They were easily hunted down by the Germans. With few weapons, they rarely could stand and fight. Their main problem was that neither of the major Polish partisan organizations (Nationalist and Communist) would accept them as allies against a common enemy. To a lesser degree, this also applied to the Russian partisans. The difference was that the Polack gentiles, when they weren't too busy killing each other, made it a point to murder any Jewish partisans the Germans had missed. This is another thing for which I can't forgive my former countrymen.

It was in mid-December 1942 that the *Judenrat* was told that everyone in the ghetto was being transferred to Germany to work as labourers. Actually, when we received notice that our names were included in the first transport of 3,000, we were optimistic about our futures. Even Mother, who was by this time emaciated, thought we might be better off in a labour camp. She said, "At least we'll have our daily bread, and soup, and things like that. They're not going to let us starve in a *labour* camp." Consequently, we were filled with anticipation the night a convoy of about fifty peasant sleighs arrived at the ghetto gate to begin our transfer through the deep snow to a railway siding beyond the town where a "train" now awaited our departure. (Actually, each horse pulled two small, open sleighs, which between them carried, maybe, thirty people jammed together.) Because we were allowed only one small parcel of personal belongings each, we were putting on three shirts, two coats, three pairs of pants, socks, whatever we had, in order to take everything with us. To carry food for our journey (we were told to take enough for two days), we'd purchased some heavy cotton bags on the black market that, cruel irony, had been

Transport to hell.

Red Army issue for carrying gas masks.

I suppose we might have been forewarned of lurking evil by the fact that we were herded onto the sleighs in rather brutal fashion by *SS* troops, instead of in the strictly disciplined manner of the Polish guards or *Wehrmacht* soldiers to whom we'd become accustomed at Pruzany. And perhaps my father was. But as we travelled through the town and into the countryside, and saw all the homes that had been decorated for Christmas, and trees with white candles glowing into the dark beyond their windows, all I thought about was the people inside, sitting by their warm fires, eating good food and fruits and preserves. And I puzzled yet again over why gentiles were free to live their lives and celebrate their holidays when we were not, before my mind turned to our unknown destination, and what might actually await us there. I was apprehensive, and a little excited. I'd never ridden on a train before. Then, as a light snow began to fall, my mind went blank, and I just listened to the jingle of the horse's harness, and to the muted sounds of whatever conversation Father was having with our White Russian driver — until my reverie was broken by the sudden din of revving truck engines and fiercely barking dogs.

CHAPTER III

FREEDOM THROUGH WORK

As sound became sight, I was terrified. I assume Lenka and Aleksei felt the same. Mother was in shock. Only Father seemed capable of any movement as frenzied *SS-Einsatzgruppe* killers began to flail us with their whips, and wild Alsatian attack dogs strained at their leash-ends for our throats. To the screams of *"Schnell, schnell, schnell,"* the inmates of the Pruzany ghetto were driven from the sleighs that had delivered them into the waiting freight and cattle cars. It was Father who organized us into sitting positions along the back wall of what was to become a rolling dungeon. Father, Mother, Lenka, me, Aleksei: our battle order, as we fended off those other poor creatures who attempted to intrude physically on this last small space on earth the Mielnicki family would ever share.

Our wooden boxcar filled to capacity, its door slammed shut and locked from the outside, its inhabitants sorted out to the best of their ability, the weeping, wailing, shouts, and curses finally stilled. I don't remember how many we were in total. A hundred, maybe more. Whatever our number, we sat in stunned silence, hardly daring to think, lest we acknowledge what each of us knew to be true: we were about to be murdered by our German captors.

And that particular moment, however long it actually lasted, was as good as this journey into hell was going to get. No one as yet had urinated in one of the corners, peed or shat in their pants, vomited all over him or herself or a neighbour, or died. All these things we had to look forward to as the train began to rock forward down the tracks. (The only vile essence experienced by others who were transported to the death camps that we didn't inhale was chlorine, which the SS often used, theoretically as a disinfectant in its freight and cattle cars, but in reality to kill as many of its "passengers" as was possible by causing respiratory failure during the trip. Still, the stink of caged humanity is something that must be experienced to be believed.)

I did not know how long we'd been on the train when we finally reached the ramp at Auschwitz-Birkenau, and I do not know today. It had to have been longer than two days, because we ran out of food and water. It could have been three days. It could have been seven. It could have been anywhere in between. Ours was an environment in which time lost all meaning. For sixteen or seventeen hours out of every twenty-four, it was so dark that you couldn't see your hand in front of your face. For the other seven or eight, when streaks of pale light filtered through the two tiny, open (except for the barbwire) windows, located on either side of the door, everything was so foggy from the mixture of human breath and freezing air that you barely recognized the members of your own family. And like everyone around us, we soon drifted into a near-permanent state of blessed semi-consciousness. Awakening was like a bad dream. You'd be chilled to the bone. Your arms and legs would be asleep. But you couldn't stand up, because to do so was to invite someone else's feet and legs into your vacated space. Fistfights were not uncommon when this occurred. All you could do to restore circulation and warm your body was to push away gently the sister or brother who'd fallen asleep against you, adjust the position of the parcel of clothing on which you'd been sitting, rub yourself all over, and maybe eat a little

Main gates, Birkenau.

bread, if you still had some. Oblivion was our only real respite from the never-ending pain, and from the thoughts we didn't want to think. I was so far out of it that I didn't even know that only an arm's length away my mother was dying.

We had stopped so many times en route, to be shunted here or there as military trains headed for the front passed us by, that I'd ceased to pay attention. Consequently, I had no idea that we'd actually arrived anywhere, when we bumped once more to a halt. That is, until the door to our dark and fetid transport suddenly was thrown open, and we were driven out with clubs and whips and snarling German wolfhounds, just as we'd been driven in. As those of us who still were able stumbled forth into the blinding glare of artificial lights, we were forcibly separated into two groups: women and children in one, men in the other. Father was beside me on the ramp, as was Aleksei.

Instinctively, however, I knew that neither could protect me now. Undoubtedly, the lightheadedness that comes from prolonged hunger and a general disorientation also contributed to my terror, which had reached a level mere words cannot describe. I wondered, "How are they going to kill me? Are they going to shoot me? Are they going to throw me half-dead into a grave and cover me with mud?" Before I could figure any of this out, a man in a striped prisoner's jacket (from the Birkenau *Kanadakommando* — the work party that collected and warehoused all the material possessions of the new arrivals — as I was later to discover) attempted to take away my battered parcel of clothes. When I resisted, he said, "Drop it. You don't need it. We'll bring it back to you." My name was written on it, so I let him throw it on the heap of valises and parcels he and his colleagues had gathered from the people in our transport.

I don't know why this guy took pity on me, but when I asked him where we were, and what was going on, he didn't try to reassure me with another lie. He was taking a big chance in not saying, "Don't worry, it's just a work camp. You'll all be well treated here." I know now that he would have been shot if one of the *SS* guards had heard him mutter, albeit in a voice that the three of us caught clearly enough: "You've come to a place where the men and women who are fit will work. The rest will go some place else, *permanently.*" I understood. I guess my father and brother did as well, although I don't recall either of them saying anything. Indeed, I have no memory of any last words my father may have spoken to me.

In the meantime, the selection of those to be immediately gassed and burned had begun. Or, more accurately, the selection

Women to the left; men to the right — beginning the selection of who should live and who should die.

of that small percentage of those who would *not* be immediately gassed and burned. They were not calling out: "Doctors, engineers, accountants, over here; electricians, plumbers, carpenters, over there." It was no such thing. We'd been pushed into a ragged line by the *SS-Totenkopfverbände* guards and their snarling, barking hounds so that we might file past that night's ramp selection officer, an *SS-Unterscharführer* (Sergeant) in his mid-twenties. We were about thirty paces away when I first saw him. I hate saying anything about this son of a bitch that sounds even vaguely complimentary, but he cut an imposing figure, standing there, cane in hand, with his rather prominent chin jutting over the wide collar of his smartly tailored and obviously very warm, black *SS* greatcoat. For a second or two, he imperiously considered each of the bedraggled and shivering Jews who came before him, deciding, according to whatever diabolical criteria he employed, who would be saved for death some other day.

One disdainful look, and, by a flick of his wrist, he directed Aleksei to a group of mainly younger, healthy men in their twenties and early thirties who were being organized into ranks of five near the gate to a complex of brightly lit buildings. Then it was my turn. My heart ceased to beat. I had the feeling that this was the stop that ends my life, but I snapped to attention (as I had been taught in the Communist party Pioneers). To my utter surprise and absolute relief, I was sent to join my brother. When my father (who was still physically fit, and looked it despite his grey hair) tried to follow me on his own, however, this *Unterscharführer* caught him around the neck with the crook of his cane. "On the side, you dirty Jew," he screamed, as he pulled Father back, and began to smash him across the head.

Such was this NCO's sudden, and somehow incongruous rage that I stopped dead in my tracks, frightened that he might kill my father then and there. I suspect that the only thing that prevented him from doing so was the fact that his superiors expected him to finish his "selection" without creating any reason for mass prisoner resistance on the ramp. Whatever the actual case, stop he did, leaving the task of forcing my father to move along with the bulk of the prisoners to one of the SS dog-masters and his feral charge. When last I saw him before I stumbled numbly to Aleksei's side, Chaim Mielnicki, "bloody, but unbowed," had "not winced nor cried aloud." It was a scene of less than a minute's duration, but it has haunted my memory in every aspect of its "slow-motion" detail for more than fifty years. Yet all that I could tell my brother at the time was: "Our father didn't make it."

An hour or so later, stripped of my ragged clothing, I was waiting in line to be deloused, when this same *Unterscharführer* entered the inmates' induction block. Although the very sight of him scared the hell out of me, I doubt he seemed unduly menacing to anyone else in our lineup. No one around me, including Aleksei, had seen him beat my father. At worst, they might have thought him a typical SS. Not that this was any great consolation. They were inhuman by definition, and we were prisoners of the SS. But, as I indicated above, this fellow at least had a military bearing. And because he looked good, as he stood there leaning on his cane, surveying *his* pick of that night's transport-crop, I think my colleagues were deceived into thinking that they were relatively safe in his presence.

That is, until one of our number, a man somewhat older than the rest who'd been rather slow in undressing, made a grovelling gesture towards him and proffered what appeared to be a very fine, gold, antique pocket watch, the engraved front cover of which he opened for this Nazi-Sergeant's inspection. I didn't hear what this prisoner actually said. Maybe he was trying to trade his obviously valuable timepiece for his freedom, I don't know. Whatever it was, the *Unterscharführer* took the watch by its gold chain and swung it against the wall with all his strength. And against the floor, again and again with maniacal fury, until its works fell out and scattered around the room. The half-naked prisoner stood there dumbfounded. Then, as he had done to my father, this Nazi version of "Dr. Jekyll and Mr. Hyde" began to smash this utterly defenceless Jew across the head and face with the heavy handle of his cane. I don't know how many times he hit him. We were ordered not to look. That, of course, did not prevent us from hearing the punishing *thwack, thwack, thwack* of polished wood attacking human flesh and bone, a sound that seemed to continue long after the screams had ceased. I retched such bile as my empty stomach contained when I glanced at the unrecognizable, bloody pulp of the prisoner's face as he was dragged from the induction block, never to be seen or heard of again. His assailant, however, looked like a man who had just had an orgasm. *Welcome to Birkenau.*

Although I had now twice observed it, it would take me a while longer to understand that, in most circumstances, the SS guards would never touch a prisoner with their hands. It was always with their canes or sjambok-like whips. Their reason: fear of lice. Because the humble louse knew no discrimination — it didn't care whom it infected, whether Nazi German or Polish Jew, with dread disease — the SS took extreme precautions against it. Thus, delousing and showering new arrivals was not enough, every hair on our bodies had to be clipped to a millimetre's length to deny a home to any future lice — an hygienic combination that would be repeated weekly until I got to Bergen-Belsen in 1945.

It was while this was happening to me in the Birkenau induction block that I asked my inmate "barber" who the *SS*-Sergeant with the cane was. He shushed me, then mumbled in reply: "A Nazi son of a whore called Kuhnemann. Look out for him. He's a rotten, evil, thieving asshole, who should go back where he came from inside his mother." When I asked him if he knew where my father and mother were, he advised, "Forget about your parents. They're being burned. They were gassed, and now they are being burned." I don't know that I actually believed him, and this must have shown on my face, because he continued, "This goes on day and night here. They're going to kill all the Jews in Europe. If ever they win the war, there will be no more Jewish people." He quit talking when one of the other *SS* guards approached, and got back to the business end of his hand clippers, making certain that he met his quota of shaved bodies per hour, lest he join the next batch of prisoners headed for their lethal shower and the enormous pyre of logs beyond. (The infamous ovens and high chimneys of the Birkenau crematorium had yet to be completed in December 1942.)

I still don't know how I didn't lose my mind during those first few hours at Birkenau. Standing there naked, except for my boots, looking like some kind of plucked chicken, and sustained only by adrenaline, I might have thought that I'd entered the seventh circle of hell. That is, if I'd known Dante's work, I might have. As it was, I could barely accept that the prisoner with the gold watch had been beaten to death in my presence, never mind understand that over ninety percent of the three thousand people who had travelled with us from Pruzany (many of whom I had come to know and like over the past fifteen months) had been murdered, and that my beloved parents were included in their number. I would learn from experience that something happens in the brain to short-circuit physical pain beyond a certain level so that you don't feel it anymore. Perhaps the same thing happens with emotional distress. The first time the reality of my situation seemed to sink in was a couple of weeks after our arrival.

Aleksei and I, along with hundreds of other recent internees, were in "quarantine" in what was to become the Gypsy *Lager* (compound) at Birkenau, awaiting integration into the camp's general workforce. What the *SS*'s organizational problem was, if there was a problem even, I don't know. At any rate, our quarantine, which I think lasted about eight or ten weeks, was something like a military boot camp for the eternally damned. It was where I learned the rules, the regulations, and the ropes of the deadly régime that would rule my life for the next two and a half years. As I started to say, I'd been there for maybe two weeks, when one afternoon when we weren't standing to attention in our ranks of five, while being counted and recounted, or being lectured on the evils of lice, or marched up and down or doing calisthenics in the mud and freezing rain, or on some block or compound clean-up *Kommando*, I did something stupid that irritated my brother. Whatever it was, and I no longer remember, he slapped my face. I started to cry. I said to him, "So you are my father now." At which point, he started to cry. And then we hugged, for we knew that on earth we had but each other.

In those first few hours at Birkenau, after I'd been told about my parents, was I also worried about what had happened to Lenka? I suppose I must have been. She'd been barely functional for a year and a half. Had she gone with Mother to be gassed and burned? Or was she too standing naked, waiting her turn to be shaved? When months later I chanced to see one of these female lineups, I was surprised, although I shouldn't have been, that their inmate "barbers" were male. I now know that these men sometimes were ordered to do female body searches as well. The *SS* seldom missed an opportunity to deny our people their human dignity. So far as my initial thoughts about Lenka are concerned, however, the truth is that I don't remember any of them. What I do recall is how almost deliriously happy I was a few months later, when I discovered that she was alive and working as a nurse in the so-called hospital (which not only didn't have medicines, it didn't have running water) in the women's section of the camp. She arranged for me to catch sight of her once when my duties took me to the edge of their *Lager*. I remember she was wearing a white bandanna with a Red Cross on it around her head. I felt proud that she was my sister. And when, on another occasion, Lenka somehow managed to have one of the male prisoners smuggle me a half kilo of white bread, I treasured this, savouring only a few crumbs every day until it was gone. Then, I lost all contact with her until after the War. For nearly three years, I didn't know if she was alive or dead.

Lenka, of course, has her own tale to tell, and even if I knew all its dreadful detail, which I don't, it would be wrong of me to relate here experiences that properly belong to her. That said, the one thing important to my story that she did tell me a few years ago is that our mother was so close to death when we arrived at Auschwitz-Birkenau that she had to be removed from our freight car on a stretcher. After that my sister never saw her again. When I heard this, I took consolation in the thought that Mother had died on the ramp at Birkenau, and thus missed the agony of being gassed with Zyclon B. But in writing all this down, I find myself forced to ask: what if she were in a coma, or simply too weak to stand? The answer is that she would have been added to the large pile of corpses collected from our transport, carted to the pyre, stripped of her clothing, and thrown live onto the flames. Obviously, I don't know what happened, but I suspect that Lenka avoided telling me about this for over forty years because she too had considered the alternative possibilities and their relative probability, and wanted to spare me her distress.

As I've said, it's difficult even to estimate the psychological effect of losing your nearest and dearest in such brutal circumstances. I was just a kid. At fifteen, I was one of the youngest prisoners in the quarantine compound. Such little experience as I'd had in life, I've described already. I'd never dated a girl, been to a dance, or really done anything on my own. No doubt my experiences in the ghetto at Pruzany had made me in some ways old for my age, but I was hardly mature. What is more, I was scared shitless. I think I probably would not have survived those first two months had I not had my brother by my side. As I intimated in an earlier chapter, Aleksei and I had become inseparable — the large death camp numbers tattooed on the outside of our left forearms were 98039 and 98040, respectively. These numbers became our official names, and our personal distinctions (later arrivals had their numbers — smaller in size, with alphabetical prefixes — tattooed on the inside of their forearms) for the duration of our internment. I also said that in Birkenau Aleksei quite literally was singing for our lives and our suppers.

———

Kuhnemann, Heinrich Johannes Kuhnemann: this *SS-Totenkopfverbände* ramp officer who had sentenced my father to be gassed and burned. This demonic sadist who had savagely murdered the half-naked Jew with the gold watch. This cold-blooded Nazi killer who, a week or two later, and without so much as a change of expression, assassinated one of my high school friends from Bialystok. This latter crime occurred one evening when the three hundred or so prisoners with whom we shared "accommodation" were standing rigidly to attention in the roadway outside our block (barracks) for roll call and inspection, which was being taken by an *SS-Untersturmführer* (Second Lieutenant) and Kuhnemann. Yossele, my former classmate, was standing in the front rank. I was directly behind him. Whatever possessed my friend I can only surmise, but when the Lieutenant paused in front of us, Yossele, instead of doffing his cap as required, slapped the *SS* officer's face. Whereupon, Kuhnemann calmly drew his

The SS-Totenkopfverbände guard at Auschwitz-Birkenau.

pistol and shot this boy at point-blank range. Had his revolver not been a small calibre particularly suited for summary executions, the bullet would not have lodged in Yossele's skull, and he would have murdered me as well. In the ranks of the prisoners, nobody moved; and Kuhnemann and the *Untersturmführer* continued their count as if nothing had happened. I remember looking down on Yossele's body as it lay across my feet, staring at the bullet hole just above his nose, and wondering why so little blood was exiting from the wound. It may have been no more than my fevered imagination, but it seemed to me that Yossele had a smile on his lips.

I earlier mentioned Aleksei singing for our suppers: obscene contradiction though this may appear, Heinrich Kuhnemann, in addition to being a certifiable psychopath, was a *music lover.* Indeed, he would go on to a highly successful career in German opera after the War (under the assumed name of *König*). At Birkenau, *SS*-Sergeant Kuhnemann used his position of authority to audition singers among the prisoners, which is how Aleksei came to his attention. Kuhnemann was so impressed with Aleksei's voice that he would come to our barracks-block maybe twice a week in the afternoon or early evening to have my brother perform: German songs, Polish songs, Russian songs, French songs, even Jewish songs — eventually everything that Aleksei had ever known. This was purely for Kuhnemann's personal pleasure and enjoyment.

He would arrive. The block would be cleared of other prisoners, except for Aleksei and me. For reasons that I never thought to question, my presence was an accepted part of this arrangement. The *Blockältester* would hurry to provide him a chair. Kuhnemann would make himself comfortable. Often he'd sip from the bottle of vodka that he seemed always to carry. And my brother would sing. Me, although this wasn't always possible, I tried to stay out of sight. There was never anything about Kuhnemann that didn't frighten me half to death, including having him look at me with his cold blue eyes. I have no reason to believe that this *SS*-killer knew that he'd sent our father to his death. Nor do I have any reason to believe that if he'd known he would have cared. We certainly never told him, not that we were allowed to speak to him unless he spoke to us first.

Our reward for Aleksei's performances was an extra two-litre bowl of soup each day from the bottom of the container where the barley was the thickest. Kuhnemann saw to it that we each were issued with warmer clothes, including extra woollen undershirts, and ones that actually fit (as opposed to the random sizes we received on our arrival). We were also excused from many of the afternoon and evening work *Kommandos*. And because it was known that we had Kuhnemann's protection, the *Kapos* in charge of the work parties and the other prisoners with authority over us (all of whom, initially at least, were older gentile Poles or Russians, who had been in Birkenau for at least a year), such as our block elder (*Blockältester*) and his deputies, the block section supervisors (*Stubedienst*), tended not to give Aleksei and me a rough time. Physically, this got us off to as good a start as was possible in that hell, where the official SS policy was to work and starve its prisoners until their usefulness was expended. Mentally, this helped me to recover somewhat from my initial trauma. While it lasted, our inmate colleagues may have been resentful of our good fortune, but they had no choice but to accept it. Besides, Aleksei insisted that we always keep some of our extra ration for one or other of the men who shared the wooden shelf on which we slept at night.

In any event, our "privileged" existence came to an end after about two months when Aleksei developed water on the knee, the one that he had injured in his swimming accident years before in Wasilkow. In the men's camp at Birkenau, there was not even the equivalent of the "hospital" in which our sister worked. If you cut yourself, you had to pray that your urine was sufficient to clean the wound, and that the blood would congeal quickly, because the most that you could get from the camp central infirmary was a thin paper bandage. Death sentences were automatic for those prisoners who showed any sign of serious injury, illness, physical deficiency, or lice. My God, I once saw a prisoner sent to the crematorium for having boils on his neck. The point is that in any circumstance other than ours, Aleksei would have been part of the next "selection" of those from inside the camp to be gassed and burned.

Instead, Kuhnemann ordered him sent by ambulance to the hospital in Auschwitz I, where he had *some chance*, although, as I later would discover, *not a great chance* of survival. (At the time, we didn't know anything about the "medical" experiments of the SS "doctors," or the lethal phenol injections that patients often received in lieu of treatment.) There was, and perhaps still is, a hierarchy of horrors among the Holocaust survivors. In Birkenau (which was also known as Auschwitz II), we thought those in Auschwitz proper (or Auschwitz I) had it soft. Of course there was strict discipline, hard labour, corporal punishment, and public hangings at Auschwitz, where the *SS* guards and *Kapos* were also free to beat and murder prisoners as they chose, but it was not a death camp *per se*. Birkenau was *the* death camp. Auschwitz, brutal though it may have been, was a concentration camp. Auschwitz prisoners, or the Christian ones at least, received food parcels from relatives full of black bread, salamis, and large onions. When officials from the International Red Cross came on inspection tours, they were shown Auschwitz, where the inmates had clean clothes and bedding (some even had sheets), and, in periods when it was not too crowded, individual bunks. They were never shown Birkenau, where laundry facilities were nonexistent (we were issued "new" clothing every month or so, but it was never clean, merely deloused), and where we each had one thin blanket to wrap ourselves in at night — seven men on their thin sleeping pallets, crammed against each other for warmth (and because we had no choice) on each level of our three-tiered, multi-banked bunks. Auschwitz even had a brothel, where for a Reichsmark gentile prisoners could avail themselves of carnal delights with women who'd been sentenced for various criminal offences. In Birkenau, we could only talk about pleasures of the flesh. God knows, we got erections, but, at night, we were always too tired even to dream.

The curious thing is that in my heart I had accepted Kuhnemann's word that my brother would receive appropriate medical attention, even though I knew that they often used the ambulances to take people directly to the gas chamber. Consequently, although more than merely anxious about being left to my own devices for however long Aleksei might be in hospital, I was also extremely happy that day in February 1943, when he limped to the waiting ambulance for the two and a half kilometre ride to Auschwitz. I remember saying to Aleksei as we parted, "I hope to see you soon." I also remember bursting into tears. Heaven knows, I desperately wanted him back at my side. It never occurred to me that our separation might begin the tortuous path to his own survival. Several months passed before I learned that the operations (really experiments by Nazi medical students) on Aleksei's knee had proved successful enough to get him walking and working again. We had no means of communication. The only Jews who were allowed to write letters were Nazi collaborators, who wrote glowing reports about the conditions at Auschwitz to allay the fears of those about to be transported from Western Europe. I found out that Aleksei had become a male nurse in the Auschwitz hospital when one of the people with whom I worked came in contact with him and recognized that the number on Aleksei's arm was one digit short of mine. My colleague said, "98039, eh? So, you know my friend Mendel." That, however, was our last contact for nearly fifty years.

———

Literally thousands of books, articles, and documentary films have been written or produced over the years about Auschwitz, and the atrocities committed there — somewhere between 1,600,000 and 2,000,000 people murdered, 90 percent of whom were Jews — that I think it safe to assume the reader will have already a suffi-cient idea of its location, physical layout, the nature of the *SS* régime, etc., without this information being repeated in any great detail here. What is often confused in the public mind is that within its forty square kilometres there were three related but separate *SS* entities: 1) the concentration or prison camp, AUSCHWITZ I, where the prisoners wore striped uniforms; 2) the death camp for the mass extermination of European Jewry, AUSCHWITZ II or BIRKENAU, where the prisoners wore civilian clothes; and 3) the prisoner compound at MONOWITZ or AUSCHWITZ III, from which the *SS* contracted out Jewish and Slavic slave labourers (in striped uniforms) for the equivalent of sixty cents a day to BUNA, the I.G. Farben company's giant methanol and synthetic rubber works. "Extermination through labour" was the *official* name for this Nazi policy.

In combination, Auschwitz was a huge operation. My Polish Catholic friend Sigmund Sobolewski (a survivor who was imprisoned in Auschwitz I from June 1940 — his number was 88 — until just before its liberation by the Russians in January 1945, and who has campaigned tirelessly for an official Polish recognition of the Jewish sacrifice there) estimates its average prisoner population in July 1944 at 155,000. To give this some comparative relevance, he likes to point out that Penticton, British Columbia, an average North American town that is also forty square kilometres in size, houses slightly more than 33,000 people. What my dear friend doesn't say is that 120,000 of those July 1944 prisoners would have been within the few square kilometre confines of Birkenau, which throws his comparison into a cocked hat. Oxford historian Alan Bullock in his *Hitler, A Study in Tyranny* notes that, "In forty-six days during the summer of that year [1944], between two hundred and fifty thousand and three hundred thousand Hungarian Jews alone were put to death at the camp and the SS resorted to mass shootings to relieve the pressure on the gas chambers." Bullock's figures may be conservative. Auschwitz *Kommandant*, *SS-Obersturmbannführer* (Lieutenant Colonel) Rudolf Höss, in his affidavit at Nuremberg in April 1946, testified to executing 400,000 Hungarian Jews in the summer of '44. Whatever the actual number, Auschwitz, to use writer Philippe Aziz's words (from his *Doctors of Death, Volume Two*), was "an immense metropolis: the metropolis of death."

―――――

What I remember most is not the crowding, but the chimneys at Birkenau. The five towering cremation-oven chimneys. Their oily smoke. You could always tell when they were burning a transport of Jews from cities in the West. Flames shot high from the top of the chimneys, and the billowing smoke hung longer over our heads, because they had more body fat than the half-starved Jews from the Polish ghettos. My people only produced a flat yellow smoke. Not even sparks. I've never been able to get these images out of my mind. Nor have I got out of my nose the particular odour of burning human flesh that permeated the air for miles around. Sometimes, if my wife and I are having a barbecue in the backyard and I smell the chicken skin as it begins to curl and blacken over the coals, I feel dizzy and nauseous. To me, those chimneys are the sign and symbol of every vile and unspeakable thing that I have ever experienced or witnessed in my life. I associate them with the deaths of my parents and the desecration of their remains, even though I know that the bodies of my mother and father were burned in December 1942, along with thousands of others, in one of the log-filled trenches the "special" work party or *Sonderkommando* used for this purpose in the birch woods (thus the name "Birkenau") beside the camp. I know this well, as I do that their ashes were later dumped in the Vistula River. I even worked on the construction *Kommando* that dug the base for one of these chimneys, which was a job that brought me as close to joining my parents as I would come in Birkenau.

———————

I went into a state of profound depression when Aleksei was taken to the hospital in Auschwitz. As the younger brother, I'd done whatever my older sibling said I should, gone where he'd gone, followed his example. I no longer had either Aleksei's protection, or Kuhnemann's patronage. No one was ever going to give me an extra ration of soup to listen to the sound of my voice. I was still a growing boy, and I knew that a diet of 175 calories a day was not going to keep me alive. Hungry all the time, I began searching the half-frozen quarantine compound for edible roots and wilted stems. Dandelions. Chick weed. Plantain. I ate grubs and bugs — German cockroaches when I could catch them. Why not? I knew that primitive tribes in Africa and Asia did. I snuck out of my block at night, dodging the search lights, to raid the kitchen garbage cans in search of bones that still had marrow in them. Immune already to the death of others, I furtively stole scraps of bread from the pockets of dead men. It was almost as if I could hear my father saying: "Take it, and eat it quickly before somebody beats you to it. The man may be dead, but his bread is still nutritious."

Maybe I was becoming an animal. All I knew was that I was on my own and completely vulnerable. In many ways, I still looked and acted like a little kid. So much so that one of the older German inmates with a violet triangle on his jacket grabbed me one day and started to kiss me. His breath was awful. Stuck his tongue in my mouth. Put his hand down my pants. The *Blockältester* came running out of his room when I started to scream, and chased this "chicken hawk" away. I asked myself, "How will I survive alone in a hell like this?" At fifteen years of age, I decided that I wanted to die. I wasn't alone in thinking such thoughts. Birkenau was a place where you walked on egg shells, in the sense that you never knew when you were going to get hit or shot. There didn't have to be any good reason, because, as a prisoner, you didn't have any rights. You'd been sent there to die. Our life expectancy was a maximum of two, maybe three months. A prisoner really needed a strength from I-don't-know-where to be able to cope with being treated as if he should have been gassed already. God was not the answer. We'd stopped believing in Him. And a lot of people just couldn't take it. Or see the point in taking it. The important thing, I concluded, was to exit this world without suffering, like the two or three prisoners who threw themselves against the high-tension fences every day. Or, like my friend Yossele, who provoked Kuhnemann into shooting him dead. How jealous I was of him. I thought, "Being shot is okay: it's a salvation, you're finally finished." Still, I hesitated. Even after I'd received a public beating for failing to carry out an impossible command.

In Birkenau, there were rules and regulations governing every aspect of our existence, and detailed corporal and capital punishments for any and every violation of them. This was a military establishment, and the *SS-Totenkopfverbände* that ran the concentration camps was precise about such things. Typical was my situation one night in our barracks-block just before lights-out. Exhausted as usual, and desperate to crowd into our shelves for the five or six hours rest we were allowed (sleep deprivation was another constant in our miserable lives), we were standing at attention in front of our "bunks" while the Polish *Stubedienst*, who was responsible for our section, went to report to the *Blockältester* that we were all present and accounted for. Before his departure, however, he had ordered me, "98040," the youngest and most ineffectual prisoner there, to "fall out" and take charge. Specifically, I was told to make certain that none of the other prisoners moved so much as a muscle in his absence.

Well, when the *Stubedienst* returned however many minutes later, one of our number, who'd been stricken with stomach cramps, was sitting on the sanitary pail. I'd been as powerless to stop him moving as he'd been to stop his bowels. And while my colleague sat there noisily splattering the sides of the bucket, this rotten anti-Semite dressed me down for being a "worthless and untrustworthy, goddamned little Jew," then marched me before the *Blockältester*, another Pole of similar sentiment, who sentenced me to ten strokes across my bare behind for "failing to obey the direct command of a block superior." With no fat on my bottom to cushion the bruising, I passed out after the third blow.

At least my punishment, cruel and asinine though the judgement of my "masters" may have been, was by the "book," which among other things prevented them from taking their sticks to my equally bony back. I couldn't sit down for a week, but I wasn't maimed, and I had no good reason to be afraid for my life. There were other occasions on which I was hit, but this side of the gas chamber, which represented the ultimate in terror, my greatest fears were generated by the fact that most often there were no rules governing the conduct of those with power over us. For example, I was not twenty feet away when I witnessed two older fellow prisoners murdered in the most outrageous manner imaginable — which really is saying something in a place like Birkenau. The rule was that if you had to relieve your bowels during the day, you had two minutes in which to do so. Time enough, because everyone had diarrhea, but, given our meagre diet, generally not a lot of it. (In case anyone is interested, you kept a leaf or two in your trouser pocket with which to wipe yourself. I once used poison ivy with a rather unforgettable result.)

A Birkenau toilet.

The latrines, of course, were foul in the extreme: maybe two hundred holes, back to back, over a lake of human excrement. Nevertheless, they were one of the few places of respite in the camp. A warm haven in which to eat an extra portion of bread if you'd been lucky enough to organize it. And if you gave the *Kapo* in charge a piece, he might let you stay a few minutes longer. You learned to ignore the stench. It was almost comforting compared to the smell outside. People actually chose the latrine as a place to breathe their last. Inmates who'd been reduced to skin and bones simply sat down in the latrines and died. Of course, by this time their minds had gone as well. We called these lost souls "Mussulmans" because they invariably wandered about with their thin blankets over their heads and shoulders, looking, we thought, like Moslems with prayer shawls.

In any event, the two men that I mentioned were judged to be malingering by their work-party *Kapo*, who, with the help of the latrine *Kapo*, picked them up by their ankles, dropped them head first through the holes on which they'd been sitting, and held them beneath the surface of the shit with long poles until the bubbles stopped coming through. After which, other prisoners were summoned to fish them out, hose them down, and lug their bodies to the steps of their block for evening roll call. The *SS* guards never objected when the *Kapos*, who were themselves prisoners (but not usually Jews like the rest of us), killed the men in their charge. These two *Kapos* probably received an extra ration from the sausage factory at Auschwitz for demonstrating creative management techniques.

———

Although it was not unknown for an *SS* guard to take out his pistol and shoot a *Kapo* who somehow had offended him, it is important to observe that the *SS* could not have run the camp without the active and enthusiastic cooperation of the *Kapos*, the *Blockältesters*, and their respective deputies, the *Vorarbeiters* and the *Stubedienst*, most of whom were serving eight-, ten-, twelve-year concentration camp sentences for their convictions as thieves and gangsters. Generally, there was a camaraderie among the *Kapos*, the *Blockältesters*, and the *SS* guards. They drank vodka together. They murdered Jews together. And sometimes they buggered little boys together. Many *Kapos* and *Blockältesters* had as their personal servants *"pupils"* (which in Polish slang means a teacher's pet or "brown-noser") from among the twelve- to fourteen-year-olds who had somehow been missed in the initial "selection" on the ramp. Someone to clean their boots, do their laundry, run their errands, and, if these criminals' tastes ran in that direction, to be their "wives."

And, naturally enough, I suppose, a great number of these felons were anti-Semitic to the core, the worst of whom, in my experience, were the Slovaks. They hated Jews and they hated Poles, and a lot of us were both. In fairness, however, my *Blockältester* at the time of the above double murder was a Jew from Warsaw, albeit a French citizen (whatever that might prove) by the name of Pinkus, who was as brutal a man as you could find. He ran one of Birkenau's three brick barracks-blocks, and seemed in competition with the *Blockältesters* of the other two for the camp super-beast title. He was hanged in Paris after the War for all his "good" deeds

One of the few truly bright spots during my time in Birkenau involved the death of a particularly savage *SS* officer at the hands of a reputedly alluring dancer from Warsaw by the name of Horowitz. This was not something I witnessed. Friends in the *Sonderkommando* told me what happened. What I personally experienced was the punishment imposed on the entire camp for her heroism: two days of doing pushups in the mud — which I would gladly do again for the privilege of recounting her story.

Apparently the *SS* officer responsible for supervising the gassings that day, an *Obersturmführer* (Lieutenant) by the name of Schillinger, liked what he saw as he and the other *SS* in his command were collecting the rings, watches, and other pieces of jewellery worn by the women who'd disembarked from that day's transport. There was nothing subtle or patient about Schillinger. The women and children who surrounded him had all been marked for death — an occasion for which they would all be undressing momentarily. Instead of waiting, however, he walked right up to the Horowitz woman and told her to take off her clothes; he wanted to see how far up her legs went. Backed her into a corner.

I don't know what else he had in mind. Possibly rape, although this was theoretically against the Nazis' racial laws. More likely, humiliation, and maybe a little torture for good measure. He was another one of these tall, handsome, young Germans, who, in an instant, could turn into a slavering beast. These people enjoyed pain, as long as somebody else suffered it. And Schillinger's record was worse than Kuhnemann's when it came to beating people to death. Certainly, he was accustomed to being obeyed, and capable of anything, even with hundreds of about-to-be-dead women and children watching. Possibly he thought this would make a good story to share with his fellow officers over a schnapps or two at the end of the day.

Whether the willowy dancer from Warsaw had already figured out that the room next door was a death chamber is anybody's guess. One thing, however, is certain: she was not about to satisfy the lascivious or sadistic desires of any *SS-arschloch* without a fight. Appearing ready to obey his command, she reached down to remove her shoes, but instead filled her hand with some of the decayed mortar that had fallen from the concrete-block walls of the gas chamber anteroom. Then, suddenly, she stood up, threw the sand into Schillinger's eyes, reached forward, snatched the pistol from its holster on the front of his belt, and pumped three bullets into his chest and stomach. Schillinger collapsed at her feet, not yet dead, but close.

When *SS* Sergeant Emmerich came charging to his superior's rescue through the throng of screaming women and children, she shot him in the arm. Emmerich turned tail and fled. Other women from the transport then charged the guards at entrance to the changing room, and secured its control, severely injuring two more of the *SS* with their bare hands in the process. By the time Camp *Kommandant* Höss and a squad of heavily-armed *SS* blasted their way back in, Schillinger was beyond help. He was to die from his wounds in the ambulance en route to the hospital at Auschwitz I.

Nothing like this had ever happened at Birkenau before. Flags were at half-mast. You'd have thought Germany had lost the War, as the *SS* went into mourning over the loss of their "valiant" comrade, "killed in action." Personally, I'd have laughed out loud at them, even through the pain of the pushups, if I hadn't known that the penalty for doing so was also instant death.

At the time, and for more than fifty years thereafter, until I read the very brief account of this incident in Sir Martin Gilbert's 1985 book, *The Holocaust: A History of the Jews of Europe During the Second World War*, I didn't even know Madame Horowitz's name, or that she and all the other women and children who had survived *Kommandant* Höss's infantry charge were taken individually from the gas chamber to be shot in the back of the head — which to the *SS* mind apparently was a fate crueller than their murder through the inhalation of Zyclon B.

In the story as I originally heard it, the heroine was a Belgian actress who'd starred in Hollywood westerns during the 1930s — which seemed a reasonable enough explanation of her skill in taking Schillinger's hand gun away from him, and doing with it what the rest of us could only dream of. The important point, of course, was that hers was a tale victorious that was told and retold a thousand times by prisoners, desperate, but ultimately too tired, hungry, and despairing, to revolt.

———

It is difficult to maintain any balance when writing about one's experiences in a place like Birkenau. For example, I'd been working at the end of a shovel on the crematorium-construction *Kommando* that I alluded to earlier. This would have been in February or March of 1943. At maybe one hundred and ten or fifteen pounds, I was still wiry, but not fit for heavy labour. And these were ten-hour-a-day shifts, in which one didn't dare fool around. The Slovak son of a bitch who was our *Kapo* and his several *Vorarbeiters* were throwing bricks at you if you slowed down. From what I've read since, *Kommandant* Höss was under pressure from *SS-Reichsführer* Himmler and, more immediately from his extermination coordinator, *Sturmbannführer* (Major) Adolf Eichmann of the state security *Reichssicherheitspolizeihauptamt*, to get his killing machine into high gear to facilitate the *"Final Solution."* (I actually saw Eichmann once.)

The attitude of the *SS* staff officers at Auschwitz was that they didn't mind working their inmates to death to meet their production schedule. After all, there was an endless supply of us, and one way or the other we were all going to wind up dead. This certainly applied to the eighty or so men in the *Kommando* in which I was working. They were dropping around me like flies: from hunger, from exhaustion, from the cold, from infections, from cholera, from typhoid fever, from a hundred different things that found their final fatal expression in industrial accidents, flying bricks, and beatings. I worried that I was not only getting weaker by the day, but that my boots were beginning to rot.

Birkenau was built on swampland. Our boots or shoes had been the only part of our original clothing that we'd been allowed to keep. This may seem strange to those who have never been in a similar situation, but good footwear was an essential of survival, especially working in that half-frozen mud in the rainy winter season. And people were prepared to risk their lives for a decent pair of boots, something I learned that first night we arrived. When finally we were marched to our block and sent to bed, I was lying there with my knee-high boots still on, too tired and upset to sleep, when some other prisoners raided our quarters. I heard them

The shoes of Jewish victims.

whispering in Russian, a language I'd spoken all my life. They were after our boots and shoes. When someone grabbed one of my boots and tried to pull it off, did I ever give him a blast: "Get lost. Go to hell. You son of a whatever." He thought he was dealing with a fellow countryman, because he left me right away. Quite apart from the fact that he couldn't get my boot off, it was a matter of honour: he wasn't about to steal from another Russian. But he and his colleagues were desperate enough to risk summary execution rather than wear the camp-issue, wooden-soled clogs, which often slipped from your feet to disappear forever into the deep gumbo of Birkenau's construction sites and byways. Failing that, their cotton tops wore out. Either way, you were shoeless.

The *SS* had tens of thousands of good shoes and boots in its *Kanadakommando* warehouse (along with similar stocks of eyeglasses and children's toys — most everyone with any interest in the Holocaust has seen photographs of these obscene collections).

We didn't have adequate footwear because it suited the Nazis to have us stealing from each other. We couldn't very well organize against them if we couldn't trust the prisoners in the next barracks-block. And the fact is that we didn't trust the people in our own barracks-block. Everybody was stealing from everybody. You slept each night with your pair of boots or shoes beside your head. You knew that if your feet froze or blistered, which they were certain to do in clogs or rotted leather (socks were not part of our clothing allotment), you would have difficulty walking. The *Kapo* would beat you. If they became infected or froze severely, gangrene would set in. Then someone would "select" you.

While working on that crematorium chimney, I froze one toe so badly that I had to have the end of it removed. Without anaesthetic. Cut off. Stitched up. Wrapped in a paper bandage. And stuffed back into my sodden boot. I still remember the pain. I screamed my lungs out. (Although I later went crazy with the itch of what I could no longer find to scratch, I was lucky that I didn't get infection and lose my entire foot.) As to why I wasn't sent to meet my Maker, *SS-Unterscharführer* Kuhnemann intervened to save me from that fate. He saw me limping as my *Kommando* marched to work one morning. Summoned me from its ranks. Sent me to the camp central infirmary. And afterwards had me assigned light cleanup duties in #3-block, Pinkus's three-storey, brick chamber of horrors. Pinkus, as I've described, was a monster, a short, heavy, muscular man, who crushed heads with his cudgel like he was smashing apples. Made me pee my pants to be any-where near him, even though I knew he wouldn't touch me if Kuhnemann forbade it.

————

Was I grateful to Kuhnemann for saving my life? I suppose that when I wasn't wishing that I was already dead, I was. Basically, however, I was simply too stunned by my pain and terror to consider the question. Later, I would find it convenient to credit Aleksei, or at least his beautiful voice, for Kuhnemann's act of charity towards me. The more important question is, did Kuhnemann's conduct in saving my life and that of my brother make him any less guilty of crimes against humanity? The simple answer is "No." There is no doubt that Kuhnemann admired my brother's voice, but what he did for us was mere caprice. As an *SS-Unterscharführer* at Birkenau, Kuhnemann had the absolute power to indulge his moods, be they cruel or kind, so far as his treatment of the Jewish or other prisoners was concerned. To my knowledge, the only time he ever got into trouble was when his *SS* superiors caught him stealing from the collection of gold teeth and fillings that were removed each day from the corpses of their victims (to be melted into gold bars and deposited in Swiss Banks). The punishment for this proud product of the Hitler Youth: two weeks in the brig, and temporary demotion to *SS-Rottenführer* (Acting Corporal). No doubt this also ended any aspirations the still young Kuhnemann may have had for recommendation that he be accepted for officer training at one of the *SS Junkerschulen*.

When my friend and fellow Holocaust survivor, University of British Columbia professor Rudy Vrba, recognized Kuhnemann on stage during the performance of an opera in Duisburg, Germany, in 1989, he publicly denounced him and pressed a formal complaint about Kuhnemann's war crimes with the German authorities. When I read about this in the 2 November 1989 edition of the Vancouver *Western Jewish Bulletin*, I phoned Vrba: "Rudy, I know this Kuhnemann. He killed my father." At first, he didn't believe me. I was amazed that I had to convince him. In any event, the upshot was that I went to Frankfurt in May 1990 to tell my story to the German prosecuting attorney. When he asked me to identify Kuhnemann in a photo album containing the pictures of forty *SS* officers and NCOs, including a couple who looked vaguely like Kuhnemann, I had no difficulty. His was a face forever etched in my memory. Had I met him on the street in 1990, I would have recognized him, grey hair and all. Short of radical cosmetic surgery, there was no way to disguise the "Jay Leno" chin that I'd first seen jutting over the collar of his black *SS* great coat that December night in 1942.

The summary of his trial in *Response, The Wiesenthal Center World Report* (Fall, 1991) states that Kuhnemann (alias Heinrich König, President of the German Trade-Union Confederation) was "officially charged with five murders and with participation in over 100 others.... [He was] also accused of once ripping a baby from the arms of its mother and smashing its head against a telephone pole." I testified against him, for the prosecution, at his trial in Duisburg in June 1991, recounting all that is recorded above (including the "good" things that he did for Aleksei and me). Apart from what appeared to be a brief anxiety or slight heart attack during the first of two days of testimony (although it may have been faked — he was attempting to look old and frail to evoke such sympathy as he could from the three German judges), Kuhnemann, surrounded by his *four* lawyers, listened to what I had to say without any display of emotion. During one of the recesses, however, he approached me in the corridor outside the courtroom. He didn't say anything, but simply bowed and tipped his hat. Initially, I thought that this might be his embarrassed way of asking my forgiveness, but on reflection I think that his gestures were sardonic. He knew something that I didn't. Nearly ten years have past. His trial has not concluded. And he remains free on the equivalent of US$100,000 bail (*whatever or whomever the source of these funds*). Kuhnemann is now in his late seventies, or early eighties, too old, under German law, to be sent to jail. This *SS-criminal* will die at home, surrounded by his loving family. I don't want revenge, but I wouldn't mind a little justice after all these years.

———————

A final question is whether Kuhnemann was some sort of aberration in the ranks of the SS at Birkenau, in terms of his artistic tastes and talents. I cannot speak to their musical or other gifts, but, in my experience, there were a lot of *SS-Totenkopfverbände* personnel who, after a heavy day's work killing Jews and Gypsies, sought relaxation in entertainment provided by their prisoners. There were famous singers, musicians, actors, and athletes in our midst. We had our own orchestra in Birkenau, which played as we were marched off to work in the mornings, and when we returned at the end of the day. Under the baton of the former conductor of the National State Opera of Warsaw, they gave concerts for the SS on Sunday afternoons. And they "welcomed" those transports of new prisoners that arrived during the daylight hours, thus calming the fears of those about to be gassed and burned — a "treat" that the Mielnicki family missed. We also had a small theatre company that put on plays for the guards and privileged inmates. Then we had prisoner football teams, whose players exhausted themselves for an extra quarter kilo of bread, often injuring themselves in the process and winding up dead instead. We had boxing even, with the winners, like gamecocks, living to fight another day. The men, like Kuhnemann and Schillinger, who starved and overworked us, brutalized and beat us, strangled and hanged us, gassed and cremated us, demanded that we also provide them still *other* amusements.

And from what I've heard, these were often men who read bedtime stories to their little ones at home, listened to Mozart, enjoyed fine wines and gourmet cooking. The next day, of course, they took photographs of their crimes against the Jews for the enjoyment of their families. They were the devoted sons, husbands, and fathers, who, in order to get an extra seven days leave to spend taking their parents, or their wives and children on picnics, or to plays and concerts, would throw a piece of potato towards their camp's high-voltage, double-barbwire fence, then shoot dead the first starving prisoner who scurried forth to retrieve it, claiming that he was trying to escape. (As *SS*-marksmen, they all liked moving targets.) If Heinrich Kuhnemann and his ilk were a reasonable cross-section of the German population, then one would be forced to conclude that the Germany of Hitler and Himmler was a nation of psychotics and psychopaths. Of course, many of our guards at the lower rank level were Polish *Volksdeutsche*, Hungarians, Rumanians, and Croatians. Other nationalities may have volunteered for service in the *Waffen-SS* (as did thousands of Lithuanians, Latvians, Danes, Norwegians, Dutchmen, Belgians, Bosnians, and Frenchmen) to fight in the so-called Nazi war against Bolshevism, but those who joined *SS-Totenkopfverbände* did so in order to murder Jews and steal their gold. It was for good reason that they all wore skulls on their caps.

That said, however, the fact is that it took more than a mixed-national contingent of *SS-Totenkopfverbände* and their common-criminal helpers to run the largest death camp in the history of the world. Ignoring for a moment the human cost, its construction had involved considerable feats of engineering and organization. The sorting, disinfecting, storing, and shipping the clothing, hair, and other valuables of *two million people* was another monumental task, as was the meticulous accounting the *SS* bureaucracy demanded. Feeding the tens of thousands who made up the "permanent" inmate population of the three Auschwitz camps, however inadequate and putrid our fare, was an immense job in itself. Requisitioning wood for the pyres or fuel for the ovens, providing labour for sub-camps, farms or mines, servicing a fleet of vehicles all required care and skill. The list is endless, but only for the purpose of demonstrating that gentile thuggery was not a sufficient qualification for all the *Kapo* positions in the camp. Ultimately, the *SS* required the services of many Jews as well. These were men who seized the opportunity to survive when it was presented to them. Were they in any sense criminally culpable in the Nazi *Final Solution?* Jews like Pinkus were. However, it was my good fortune to work for two very decent Jewish *Kapos* in Birkenau, the first of whom, a rabbi from Rumania, I credit with saving many lives, mine included.

————

There were a number of us outside our barracks-block one evening after roll call. Recovered from my partial amputation, I was back slaving at the crematorium construction site. And as miserable, wet, dirty, and bone-tired as I'd ever been. We'd just been given our ration of bread (which was supposed to be a quarter kilo, but was never more than a fifth), when this man with a little goatee, and a Jewish face, came up to us. We knew he was a *Kapo* even before we saw his armband, because he was nicely dressed (in the sense that all *Kapos* had their prison clothes tailored). He picked out eighteen young prisoners, between fourteen and twenty-five years of age, and took us aside. He said, "Listen, if I can, I want to save some of you young fellows. I'm setting up a new *Wirtschaftskommando* or *Unterkunftskommando* (housekeeping or quartermaster workparty) to inventory and organize the camp's stores. Everything from spoons to sanitary buckets, fire pails to bedding and lumber for the sleeping-shelves. Everything except inmate clothing. If you're interested, give me your numbers." Which we did happily. It was up to our new *Kapo* to put everything in place for us. I, for example, could not have told my Slovak task master, "Sorry, I can't work for you today. I'm in a new *Kommando*." He would have beaten the crap out of me for my presumption. And I would have been dragged off to work for him regardless.

The next morning, as per usual, we were awakened by the *Stubedienst* at 4:30: *"Raus, raus, raus,"* he was hitting the sides of our sleeping shelves with his wooden truncheon. (You learned

Birkenau "Appellplatz", surrounded by high voltage wires.

from your very first day in Birkenau to keep your hands by your sides as you slept, lest they be broken in this morning "ritual.") Then, it was a rush to get dressed, run to the latrine, run back, splash some cold water on your face, run to form ranks of five on the muddy parade square *(Platz)*, wait to be counted *(Appell)* — thus the expression *"Appellplatz"* — which for once did not take hours, then line up back at our block for ersatz coffee (a bitter drink made from some herbs or dried vegetation, which was all we ever got for breakfast), all the time wondering, "Is this rabbi going to show up?" As good as his word, he did. We were marched off to a *warm* barracks, where we began sorting and counting pillows and blankets that had been sent over from the *Kanadakommando.*

We had always to keep busy, lest one of the *SS* guards see us slacking. In which case you would be smacked with his whip or cane. But, except for the occasional day when we had to unload trucks full of lumber for sleeping shelves, it was generally light work, and I was quick to recover from my exhaustion. We never got enough sleep, but by the third or fourth day, my muscles had quit aching. What is more, I finally had a chance to dry and clean the mud off my clothes and boots. This was important. As I've said, Birkenau was run as a military establishment. If you didn't look reasonably clean and neat, you drew the attention of the *SS* guards, the *Kapos*, the *Blockältesters*, any one, or all of whom might decide to make an example of you. Certainly, we all heaved a sigh of relief when our new *Kapo* had us transferred out of #3-block, and away from that madman Pinkus. Our new *Blockältester*, like the rabbi, was a decent human being. What is more, we had warm blankets, and had to share our sleeping-shelves with only one other person.

———

What I especially remember, however, is the first of our many noon meals in the *Unterkunftskommando*: a thick barley soup. With some pieces of meat in it! Hot. And a full litre. After working on that crematorium-chimney foundation, where we were fed three-quarters of a litre of a thin, gruel-like substance made from vegetation or herbs or poison ivy and nettles that grew along the side of the road, this was a lot. What was more, for the first time since our arrival in Birkenau, we were allowed to sit down to eat, from individual bowls, and with wooden spoons! Normally we ate standing up, two of us sharing soup from a two litre bowl. We stood facing each other, each with both hands on this container. He took a mouthful, you took a mouthful, slowly, slowly, chewing anything that might be chewable to maximize its nutritional value. A procedure that was repeated until the meal was finished. All of this done under the supervision of your *Blockältester* or *Kapo*, depending on where you were, who punished anyone who took more than his fair share. German rules required a certain etiquette even in the most barbaric of situations. I remember the rabbi (I wish I could recall his name) coming by only once as we ate, saying, as if he were our father: "Enjoying it? Good for you.

Good kids." We thought somebody from heaven had been sent to look after us. And because of this, we started to feel better about ourselves. I know that I stopped thinking about deliberately getting myself killed.

———————

It's interesting that in the company of males, sex is always a major topic of conversation, no matter how tenuous the circumstances of your existence. (And "tenuous" seems too mild a word to describe our lives in Birkenau.) I can't tell you the number of hours I spent listening to the older fellows around me boasting about the women they'd made love to, real or imagined. And in detail that left nothing to be imagined, except the actual event. Having briefly fondled three left breasts in my life, I didn't have anything much to contribute to these story-telling competitions. I just listened, fascinated. It was the same when they talked about their financial and business deals before the War. I was never with anyone substantially older than myself in the camps who ever admitted to being a failure. They'd all been successful and rich, and had screwed themselves silly every night of their lives. Bullshit to be certain, but something more than that, I think. When they stopped talking about these things, they stopped talking about life. They gave up hope, and died.

———————

I was in the *Unterkunftskommando* for about three months when our work started to wind down in about June 1943. I turned sixteen working there. It was an important time for me. The "security" (a term one uses advisedly about any situation in Birkenau) of working for the rabbi provided me the opportunity to make a transition into what one might call the main stream of camp life. It was one hell of a place to grow up, but I began to come into my own as a human being. Gregarious and helpful by nature, I started to make friends and connections. People liked me, even some of the *SS* guards, because I was quick witted and had a positive attitude. And I remembered what my father had told me about his experiences with language barriers when he was in the Austrian prisoner of war camps in World War I, where rations had also been short, barracks conditions wretched, and diseases endemic. He'd explained that if somebody's asking you for something and you don't understand, be patient. You can begin exchanging ideas with your hands. This proved good advice when it came to dealing with Gypsies or gentiles from Western Europe.

———

One of the men I became friendly with was in charge of delousing all the clothing that arrived with the transports, including that worn by the people who were immediately gassed and burned. A Polish Jew from Lodz. He had his own one-man operation. It was one of the best jobs in the camp, because the *SS* guards didn't want to go near his room. Lice. I met Mietek again in Paris after the War. A smart man, he'd gone into the shoe business — owned a couple of factories. Excellent fellow. Nice fiancée as well. We became very close friends. In Birkenau, Mietek had one of the few places that, if I could beg, borrow, or steal them in the first place, we could cook a few potatoes without fear of being discovered. Another thing that I did that was very important to my well-being was make contact with the French leaders of the Communist party cell in Birkenau. I wish I could remember their names. I do recall that one was a French prisoner of war, with an old number (smaller than mine), and that two of them were prominent in the French Communist party after the War. In fact, I went to see one of these fellows in Paris in 1946. I needed the name of a good dentist. He sent me to his. By then, of course, I'd ceased to be a "true believer." But I digress. The point is that the Communists throughout the

Auschwitz camps had their own black market connections, and knew how to look after their own.

———

As to my general deportment in the camp, I remembered what my mother had told me about the German passion for good manners, order, discipline, and uncomplaining submission to authority. Any time I was in front of an *SS* guard, I stood smartly to attention, removed my cap, and said, "*Herr Oberst*, number 98040," indicating that I was ready to listen, and was at his service. The one thing that you didn't do was cringe. You didn't resist them, but you stood up. So far as the *SS* guards responded positively to anything, it was to obedience, not cowardice. I witnessed situations where prisoners were beaten to the floor simply because they cringed. There was one *SS* guard who would occasionally butt out his cigarette half-finished and drop it for me to pick up — he actually watched to see that I was the one who retrieved it. I collected these in a little tin, waiting for the opportunity to trade with other prisoners for bits of bread or potatoes or a few grams of salt.

And twice, when working in the *Unterkunftskommando*, I faced the acid test of my mother's advice in Dr. Mengele's selection of those prisoners who would be sent immediately to be gassed and burned. *SS-Hauptsturmführer* (Captain) Joseph Mengele, wounded war hero of the *Waffen-SS*, now the *SS-Totenkopfverbände's* infamous "angel of death," as I'm sure every reader knows, was Auschwitz-Birkenau-Buna's chief medical officer, and one of the few arch-Nazi war criminals to escape capture and punishment after the War. At his selection parades, we were obliged to strip off all our clothing. As our turns came, each prisoner ran before him to be judged quick or dead. I have never forgotten the scene: I come up, click my naked heels, stand straight, and salute, "*Herr Oberst*, number 98040." Mengele, elegant and aloof in his immaculate, starched, white doctor's coat and beautiful, shiny, knee-high black boots, casts a critical eye over my thin body with its blonde fuzz and asks, *"Bist du Deutscher?"* I reply, *"Nein, Herr Oberst. Ich bin Jude."* "What a pity," he says, then smiles, "go to this side."

Which, thank God, was where my clothes were. The people who were selected for the crematorium were not allowed to get dressed again. They were loaded onto trucks, and hauled to their deaths. If I close my eyes, I can see them still. And hear them reciting a *Kaddish* as the trucks pulled away from the *Appellplatz.* The second time I came before Mengele was a few weeks later. Same procedure. I was as skinny as the first time. I raised my arm in salute, and said in effect, "Yes, Sir, here I am at your service." He looked at me, and responded, "You are here again? Good for you. Go." That was it. I thought this unbelievable. As I mentioned, you never knew, from the time you woke up in the morning until you went to bed at night, when your life or death would be determined by a superior, irrational force.

———

Because the system at Birkenau was corrupt from top to bottom, unexpected opportunities arose as well. In the midst of all that death and misery, there was a flourishing black market, in which, if you had the resources, the connections, and the nerve, you could buy most of the necessities of life. For example, I'd been working in the *Unterkunftskommando* for a month or so when one morning we received yet another load of blankets from the *Kanadakommando* warehouse. I was sorting through a pile of them when I happened on one that had thirty-six cloth-covered buttons sewn along its edges (so that a top sheet might be attached — I think not something that one often sees in North America, but common enough in Europe before the War). I didn't need anyone to tell me that it had been the property of a now incinerated Jew. And being well acquainted with the ways of our people, I immediately suspected that if this blanket had been taken on a transport to a mythical "work camp" in lieu of other clothing, these buttons might be more than they appeared. I bit a hole in the material covering one of them, and found more or less what I expected: a gold thirty-drachma coin. I had a small fortune on my hands.

I also had a problem. I had no safe place to hide my new-found wealth. I couldn't keep thirty-six gold coins on my person — large bulges in pockets got investigated. And I had no means to fashion a money belt. I knew that if I was caught with all that gold, I would be shot. It was not that I had stolen these coins from anyone, unless one regarded the *SS* as their legitimate owner — and I certainly didn't. They, however, did. Fortunately, I was smart enough to understand that some was better than none, and that if I divided it up among my *Unterkunftskommando* colleagues, collectively we would probably get away with what I didn't have the experience to handle myself. It was a perfect plan, in that there were eighteen of us, excluding our *Kapo*. The rabbi would never have gone along with my scheme. I worried that if any of us were caught, he too would be in trouble with the *SS*, but he was after all a *Kapo*, and well enough able to look after himself, I thought. I divided out the buttons. I told each one of my colleagues: "You're on your own. You do what you can. You could get a bread or two for one of those." One of our fellows had typhoid, and we used his two coins to buy aspirin, which saved his life for a while. Most in our band of brothers bought bread, although one actually managed to buy himself a broiled chicken. We compared notes on who got what. My record was the worst.

In the wooden barracks-block in which our *Kommando* was now quartered, I bunked in the same tier of sleeping-shelves as an "oldtimer" (about forty), an electrician from Paris by the name of Guttman, who put up and repaired the camp's electrified fences. I talked to him a lot. In Yiddish, the universal language of the Jewish people. At sixteen, I still needed someone to trust with my innermost thoughts and secrets. Like how, if I ever survived this hell, I would go back to Wasilkow, organize my friends, get half a dozen grenades each and machine guns, and go to the local Roman Catholic church and take revenge for the people that they killed in their pogroms, for my parents, my baby brother, and for every other rotten thing they'd ever done to us. I couldn't talk to the rabbi about these things. The Birkenau structure didn't allow it. He was a *Kapo*. And this Guttman was sympathetic, full of seemingly wise saws, and friendly to the point of saying that he'd like me to come and work with him. So I babbled on, expounding my half-baked notions on every imaginable subject. Food, of course, was my favourite topic of conversation. After nearly two years of being hungry, I was obsessed with the thought of having a full belly. My mother's cooking in Wasilkow (tzimmes and schav and gefilte fish) filled my daydreams, and gave me the saliva necessary to chew bread that was at least twenty-five percent sawdust.

Naturally, I showed Guttman my two gold coins. What was I going to do with them? he asked. "Buy bread and eggs," I replied. "If you want, I can fix that for you," he said. I knew that Guttman's son, Simon, who was also a prisoner, worked in the camp's kitchen and probably had the right connections, so I gave him one of my coins to bring me two breads. He brought one. Said stealing two kilos at once was impossible. That he still owed me one. But not to worry. In what I can only suppose was my delirium at having an entire loaf of black bread to myself, I not only believed him, I gave him my other coin to get me half a dozen eggs. I planned to eat them raw. This time, Guttman brought me nothing. He said he'd been robbed. Which was baloney.

I was mad like hell. But what could I do? Even had I wanted to, which I didn't, I wasn't big enough to force him to give me back my money. Besides, in the death camps, the *SS* guards and their convict henchmen had a monopoly on common assault. And, in the circumstances, I could hardy appeal to any of these people for "justice." Everyone involved in my drachma scam would have been hanged, or worse. I had to accept that I'd been a fool to trust Guttman in the first place. That my "soft" life in the *Unterkunftskommando* was making me so confident I'd forgotten that in the race to stay alive, it was every man for himself. The Guttmans had eaten at my expense because they needed to. And because I'd let them. I was still a kid, but I was learning.

Interestingly, I met these two in Paris after the War. They were very kind to Lenka and me. Took us out to dinner. Simon, the son, with a great bull neck and a barrel chest, had been castrated, without anaesthetic, in one of the Auschwitz "medical" experiments, so that Mengele and his quack colleagues could study the effects of this operation on us "sub-humans." And as strange as this may seem, given his condition, this young man wanted to marry my sister. Lenka, however, had other things in mind for her life. I also met the rabbi in Paris, who told me that, against all odds, seventeen of his eighteen protegés in the *Unterkunftskommando* also survived the Holocaust. The exception was our colleague with the typhoid fever.

———

A clairvoyant came over to my table when I was having lunch in a restaurant in Tel Aviv a few years ago to tell me that I had a guardian angel looking after me, whom he identified as my mother. Could this be true? I'd like it to be. Certainly, I was lucky in a lot of situations in the death camps, in the sense that I survived where others in similar circumstances died. How do you explain this? As I said earlier, almost every Holocaust survivor spends a lot of time searching for answers to this question in the particulars of his or her own experience. Destiny used to be one of my favourite explanations. That is, until I began to think about it. If, for example, destiny means that the Almighty fated me to survive, does this mean that He also decided the destruction of six million of my fellows? In which case He has a lot to answer for. Destiny is either too simplistic an answer for my purposes, or one too complex for me to understand. There is no doubt, however, that something often guided me in making the right decisions. In which case, I'm prepared to accept that this was my mother.

––––––––––

I knew, for example, when it was time to leave the *Unterkunftskommando*. I had a very strong feeling that the *SS* was going to discover that, for want of enough new work, we'd begun to recount our inventory, and that they would disband us as a result. Consequently, when I heard that the clothing workparty or *Bekleidungskommando* had lost some men to a *Kommando* of French Jews who had been sent from Birkenau to clear away the remains of the Warsaw ghetto, I approached a couple of the people I knew who worked there and asked them to introduce me to their *Kapo*. Taking the initiative in applying for a job was not the normal procedure in this land of the walking dead, but I also knew that I had to thrust myself forward if I were to continue to survive. I worked out a pitch (the reasons why this *Kapo* should "hire" me), and made certain that I was as presentable as possible (that, for example, my trousers had a good crease down the front — something achieved by placing them carefully under one's hay-filled sleeping pallet at night). I then asked the rabbi, who obviously knew the score better than I did, if I might proceed with my plan. He agreed that this would be a good thing, that the *Bekleidungskommando* was the best that Birkenau had to offer. So I presented myself to this very nice gentleman, a French Jew, who listened patiently to what I had to say. He replied, "Come in the morning, and we'll see." And so it was arranged.

I was one of about fifty people in my new *Kommando*. As usual, the hours were long. But it was easy work. Our job was to sort and examine every piece of male clothing that was to be packed and shipped to Germany. Only the good stuff. I don't know what happened to the rags the Jews from the Polish ghettos arrived in. We were getting the quality clothing, and often the blankets, from those Jews who arrived in transports from Holland, Belgium, France, Greece, Italy, which was the origin of most of the material we worked with to the end of 1943. In particular, we were charged with carefully feeling every garment for any indication that valuables had been secreted inside. A man's suit coat, for example, might have paper money hidden in its lining, gold or precious stones in its shoulder or underarm pads or sewn into its collar. Cloth-covered buttons were always suspect. In trousers, the waist bands and the cuffs made good hiding places. We each had a Gillette safety razor blade, and when we thought anything might be present, we cut open the seam, etc., to investigate. It was paper money in one big basket, gold in another, diamonds, rubies, emeralds in a smaller basket. Every day produced a small fortune for the *SS* in large denomination American bills, gold coins, and precious stones. There was a similar *Kommando* in the female *Lager*, and occasionally, when female apparel was mixed in with what we received, or vice versa, exchanges would have to be arranged. Occasionally also, or so it was attested, a congress of a more profound sort then would occur in defiance of our satanic circumstances. In other words, these quick encounters provided one of the very few chances our people ever had for normal sex. And for the rest of us to be reminded that such a thing actually existed, and to feel the eternal stirring in our trousers when we heard about it.

There was no opportunity for serious theft in the *Beklei-dungskommando*. We were supervised very closely by our *Kapo* and his two *Vorarbeiters*, as well as by one of the highest ranking officers in the camp, an *SS-Sturmbannführer* (Major), whose constant presence was an indication of the importance the *SS* attached to this final larcenous act in their meticulously planned decimation of European Jewry. The big diamonds — two, three, four carats — went straight into this *SS*-Major's leather pouch, and from there to Switzerland (or so we speculated) by special courier once or twice a week. I can't even begin to estimate how many millions of dollars passed through our hands in the seven or eight months I was there. As to the clothing we were shipping to Germany, one member of our *Kommando* was a tailor, Nitko, also a survivor, whose job it was to sew up what the rest of us took apart. I have read that the only thing the Nazis didn't manage to steal from the Jews of Europe was their life insurance. In order to collect on the policies, they would have had to issue death certificates, and thus officially document their criminal culpability in the murder of millions of innocent people. And this these cowardly black-shirted bastards were never willing to do.

I have always suspected that our *SS-Sturmbannführer* made himself a millionaire at Himmler's expense. I never had occasion to exchange a word with this man, but I often observed him in amiable conversation with our *Kapo* and the *Vorarbeiters*. As opposed to people like Schillinger and Kuhnemann, he seemed reasonably human. His passion was for fancy cowboy shirts, and Nitko our tailor spent a good portion of his time making these to measure for him, which is why I've also imagined that if he survived the War, he used his ill-gotten gains to buy a ranch in Argentina. In a place like Birkenau, everything was relative. This man was part of the *SS* machinery, but he wasn't a mean person. I never saw him abuse a prisoner. Quite the contrary, he seemed to trust us, and he saw to it that we were well treated. If Mengele was having one of his selection parades, he arranged to have us locked up in our sorting room for twenty-four hours at a time — extra shifts that he no doubt justified as essential to the German war effort. Not even Mengele could argue with that.

From a death-camp prisoner's point of view, the *Beklei-dungskommando* was paradise. Nobody was ever well fed in Birkenau (I still ate dandelions when I could find them), but the soup that was brought into us each day at lunch was thick, and we received our full litre, and sometimes more. We didn't have spoons, but we ate sitting down from individual bowls. We had ample opportunity for gossip and more serious discussion. Since this was generally in French, I learned yet another language there. We were clean. We had facilities for washing, and our own barber for shaving. We dressed almost as well as the *Kapos*, with new numbers on our smartly fitted jackets and shirts, which meant that the chances of *SS* guards or anyone else bothering us when we were on our own time were significantly reduced. If you looked like a permanent person (and we did), it meant you had a job that was important to the *SS*. In consequence, no one would give you a gratuitously rough time because that person knew that if he did, he might wind up in trouble himself. By the same token, you couldn't afford to get too cocky. You obeyed the rules. You took your cap off in salute whenever you passed an *SS* guard. And if you were wise, you kept out of sight as much as possible, stayed away from camp events, and never volunteered for anything.

I should mention that when I joined the *Bekleidungskommando*, I again changed barracks-blocks. Our *Kapo* wanted to keep us together. The *Schreiberdienst* (actually the senior *Stubedienst*, second-in-command to the *Blockältester*, and in charge of apportioning the rations, blankets, etc.) in my new quarters was a man by the name of David Druker. Yet another French Jew, he was heavily involved in the camp's black market in salamis and other food stuffs. One tough guy, he had a bad reputation for "squeezing" everyone in sight, but we became friends. Given the ease with which I was able to move around the camp, David used me as his "pickup man." Which was alright with me. I liked the idea of beating the Nazis at something more than just staying alive. No doubt I was taking an unnecessary chance, but as long as I marched smartly from point A to point B, nobody stopped me no matter what I was carrying. *SS* guards and *Kapos* alike thought I was on official business. As a consequence, I ate a little better than my *Kommando* colleagues (although I doubt I now weighed much more than a hundred pounds — I was still losing an average of a pound a month).

It's interesting the number of people that I know who actually survived Birkenau. My sister and I used to go to movies with David Druker and his wife in Paris after the War. He'd pick us up in the little Peugeot van he used in his children's clothing business. He'd made some serious enemies in the camp though. Some disgruntled survivors tried to have him convicted as a Nazi collaborator, as they had with Pinkus. Their charges, however, were unfair, and David got off. Sharp trading in the camps may have been morally questionable, but it was not a crime. The Jewish inmates in Birkenau were after all just human, with all the weaknesses in character that this implies. Jealousies arose. Quarrels ensued. Hard feelings lingered. And informers were born.

We killed those of our ilk who sold out others among us to the *SS* or their flunkies for an extra half-litre of soup. Gentiles as well. Not me. I didn't like the idea of Jews murdering Jews. Or, when it came to the crunch (my dreams of revenge to the contrary), anybody else. But I understood and accepted that my Communist colleagues had to do so when some stool pigeon was about to expose whatever minor scam they were organizing. Suffocation was best because it was difficult for the *SS* to detect. Murder by an inmate, of course, like trying to escape or "stealing" from our Nazi masters, was a hanging offence. Something that the entire inmate population was put on parade to witness on Sunday mornings — to deter the rest of us from such "crimes," as if being hanged was somehow worse than being beaten to death, shot, or gassed and burned. Only the Germans will ever understand the German mind. I should add that the *SS* always made certain that in every barracks-block there were a number of anti-Semitic Poles, Russians, Slovaks, whatever, mixed in with its Jewish prisoners. They knew full well that the resultant racial discord would encourage informers, and discourage any serious resistance to Nazi authority.

———

The *Bekleidungskommando*'s downside was that we witnessed things other prisoners only heard about. On occasion, when the *Kanadakommando* was overwhelmed with work, we had to pull a big delivery wagon down to the gas chamber to collect the clothing of those who had just been murdered. It was an awful scene when the *Sonderkommando* inmates opened the gas chamber door. (It's been replicated in the Holocaust Memorial in Washington, D.C., should anyone wish to see this.) A pyramid of dead people, who, depending on that day's humidity, may have taken anywhere up to thirty minutes to die. Men and women, who'd climbed naked one on top of the other, with children and babies pushed to the top by their mothers. I remember seeing a husband and wife who'd embraced as they died. The prisoners in the *Sonderkommando* couldn't pry them apart. So they had to break their hands. If the *Bekleidungskommando* was the best job in Birkenau, the *Sonderkommando* was the worst. One group had to pull out the bodies. Another had to cut off the hair. Another had to cut off swollen fingers to remove rings. Another had to remove any gold teeth and fillings. Another had to search other orifices for hidden Jewish treasure (which they often found). Another had to hose down the gas chamber which was full of human excrement, so that it could again pass for something other than what it was. And yet another had to move the corpses to the crematorium ovens. *"Schnell, schnell, schnell"*: there was already another transport waiting. And every time I saw all this, in my heart I cried again, "Oh, God, where are You? If You can see this, where are You?"

———

I said earlier that I no longer believed in God. Which was true. It was impossible, however, to stop being Jewish. Especially in Birkenau, where people were being systematically murdered in numbers beyond belief simply because they were Jewish. One might deny God, but it was impossible to break the bond with His people. Maybe it was the subtle influence of the rabbi in the *Unterkunftskommando*, I don't know, but at some point I started to get back to myself in terms of thinking about what it meant to be a Jew. I remember that in the *Bekleidungskommando*, we all fasted on *Yom Kippur*. Of course, fasting was a luxury. No one who was starving could afford to do that. It was, however, the unspeakable horror of the gas chamber, and the want of anywhere else to turn in the face of it, that made me call, for the first time since going into the ghetto in Bialystok, "Where are You, God? Where are You?" It was because I couldn't comprehend what I was seeing, nor understand that human beings (even German ones) could do this to each other, that I demanded the intervention of the Almighty. I wanted to scream, "Why us?" And then I became numb again.

It was only later that I began to think: Well, this is not the first time we've been persecuted. And it probably won't be the last. God made us free people, German and Jew alike. We can kill each other if we want to, and God can't do anything about it. In truth, I really didn't know if this was how the Almighty intended things to work. I couldn't have known, because it's still a mystery to me. And I guess I never will find out while I'm alive. The important thing is that I came back to God, and was the better for it. I told my work-mates, "If we don't believe that we are God's Chosen People, what do we have left?" And I became enthusiastic in the rediscovery of my faith. I was telling stories to every Jew who'd listen about how we were going to survive; that what we were experiencing was a temporary setback, citing all the *Old Testament* stories that I could remember. I didn't do this with any thought of popularity in mind, but even the *Kapos* and *Blockältesters* seemed to enjoy my company when I was beating my drum on the subject of Jewish

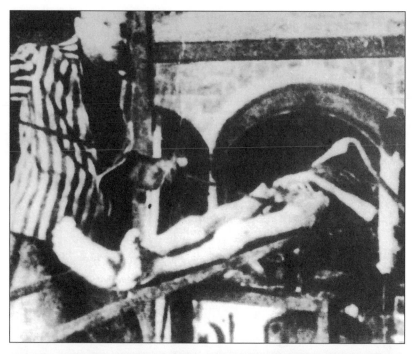

The crematorium at Birkenau.

survival. This did not stop me from attending my Communist cell meetings. There had to be some social/economic order we aspired to that was worthy of our sacrifice.

————

However, I had concerns more immediate than faith or politics when I observed a complete change in the prisoner personnel of the *Sonder-* and *Kanadakommandos*. (Thank heavens, I'd managed to secure a new pair of heavy-soled Bata boots, and a pair of socks, from one of my connections in the *Kanadakommando* before he disappeared from the face of the earth.) The *SS* did not believe in keeping alive witnesses to their crimes. In consequence, I thought it time to move on. The members of the *Bekleidungskommando* might be next. This would have been in January 1944. I'd heard a bit about the Buna industrial complex. The word was that now the construction phase was over, prisoners had a better chance of surviving there, working for the German war machine, than they did at Birkenau. There was civilian management within the I.G. Farben plants. People were better fed. Four hundred and fifty calories a day was not enough to keep anyone alive for an extended period, but it was better than Birkenau. And although regular selections took place to ship back those who had been more slowly starved and worked to death, there were no gas chambers or crematoria on the premises. What was more, there was no mud, and no road-gangs labouring to fill a never-ending series of pot-holes with large rocks so that the trucks wouldn't disappear from sight. Everything was nicely asphalted around the factories and the camp, including the *Platz*. Consequently, when I heard that there was a *Kapo* from Buna taking down the numbers of those with some technical or trade experience, I went to see him. Told him I was an electrician. I don't know that he believed me, but he put my number down on his list. When I heard it called at *Appellplatz* a few mornings later, I jumped aboard the back of a crowded truck for the *SS* prisoner compound at Monowitz, some nine kilometres down the road. I had no bags to pack. I was wearing everything that I "owned." The miracle was that I had put Birkenau behind me.

———

"Arbeit Macht Frei": I'd never seen this tribute to Nazi double-speak over the gates of Auschwitz I, although I'd certainly heard about it. It was a piece of black humour in itself, and the subject of much rude comment among the Jewish inmates: *"Arbeit Macht Frei, Krematorium Drei!"* Now, here it was again over the entrance to Monowitz: "Freedom Through Work!" You bet. There was a gallows on the *Platz* with a couple of prisoners hanging from it, lest we new arrivals misinterpret the Nazi meaning of "freedom." Joseph Borkin in his 1978 book, *The Crime and Punishment of I.G. Farben,* states that at least 300,000 prisoners passed through the Buna gates between the summer of 1942 and January 1945. I have no notion of how many of them survived to tell the tale of their experiences. I know that I almost didn't.

———

Initially, I didn't have a Buna factory job. I was part of the general labour force, assigned each morning to a different *Kommando,* or to whoever wanted me for the day. In any event, I was not long in Monowitz when, one Sunday (our normal day off), it was my bad luck to be grabbed for one of the *Lagerkommandos.* So instead enjoying a day of rest, I found myself marching down the road, a shovel over my shoulder, to clear one of the compound ditches. I didn't want to be there. I was pissed off that my boots were getting soaked. And I certainly had no intention of exhausting myself at hard labour. So I was pretending to work, bending over the shovel, moving it and my shoulders back and forth, without actually doing anything very much. Well, the *Kapo,* who happened that

SS-Reichsführer Heinrich Himmler (left foreground) inspecting "Buna-Werke" synthetic rubber and methanol I. G. Farbenindustrie. Kommandant Rudolf Höss (right foreground).

day to be the *Lager Kapo* (to whom all the other *Kapos* in the camp answered), spotted me, and began to close in. But because I was standing at the bottom of this three-foot trench, I didn't see him coming until he kicked me as hard as he could in the chest with his big boot, right over my heart. I was probably dead for a second or two. I know I passed out. Fell backwards into the slop. When I came to, he was screaming at me in German, "Pick up your shovel, you damn fool, or I'm going to kill you." But I couldn't find my shovel because my vision was blurred. I was running around in circles, like a chicken with its head cut off. Possibly he found this amusing because he didn't hit me anymore.

Obviously, I was the author of my own misfortune. I knew as well as anyone the importance of staying on your toes, and not getting too cocky — lessons I'd learned already in Birkenau — but I forgot. I was sixteen. Not that this made any difference in the death camps. The *SS* was an "equal opportunity" employer. No doubt I was lucky this *Kapo* didn't kill me. Had he kicked me again, he would have finished me off. But here was this gentile person, a Dutchman with a red triangle on his jacket, which meant that he'd been interned for being a member of the Communist party, who, in order to become one of the privileged prisoners, had not only joined the enemy, but had become one of its top killers. This I will never understand.

———

The only other incident in which my life was seriously endangered by another human being at Monowitz happened when I was working as a gardener around the *SS* barracks. This would have been in April 1944. And again, I was in some measure responsible for what happened. I was digging in a flower bed outside an open window, straining to hear a news report on the radio inside. The Red Army had just recaptured Odessa — another in a stunning series of Soviet victories that had begun with Stalingrad in January 1943, and later that year at Kursk (one of the English prisoners in our barracks-block had told me about these wonderful battles). Thinking about the fun I'd have sharing this latest report with my colleagues that evening, I'd stopped even pretending to dig. Unfortunately, I was standing there grinning from ear to ear, when one of the German officers looked out the window and saw me. I don't think he was even *SS*. Customs maybe — he had green piping on his uniform. Whatever he was, he was a genuine Nazi. He promptly marched out his barracks door, took away my spade, smashed me over the head with it, threw it at my feet, and marched away.

Blood poured down my face. It filled my eyes. I couldn't see. I thought I was dead. Somehow I managed to stop the bleeding by holding the huge piece of skin that was hanging loose at my hair-line in place with two of my fingers. That night I went to the camp infirmary. I told them that I'd hurt myself on the job, which was true enough. They patched me up. Had me come back every three days until my wound was healed. I still have the scar at the top of my forehead to remind me — not that I need to be reminded — of both the barbarism of the Nazis and the sweetness of hearing about their defeats.

————

These two incidents apart, the very fact that Monowitz had a proper hospital told me that my "decision" to move to Buna had been the right one. That, as long as I didn't try to escape, I was in fact on fairly safe ground. Indeed, when I later developed a condition in my throat (I couldn't talk) that was diagnosed as possible diphtheria, I wasn't sent back to Birkenau to be gassed and burned. I was placed under observation in the hospital's spotlessly clean isolation ward for a week. I was even fed white bread. Of course, I don't know what would have happened had I actually contracted diphtheria. But, as things turned out, I didn't. My problem went away, and I went back to serving the Nazi war machine.

Of course, perversity permeated the entire Auschwitz system. I remember one Polish prisoner who was hunted down and shot by SS guards after he had escaped from one of the *Kommandos* that were sent out at night to light fires in nearby farm fields in the hope that these would divert the bombs from Allied air raids away from the I.G. Farben industrial complex. Shot but not killed, he was taken to the Buna hospital, operated on, and nursed back to health over a period of several weeks. When he was fully recovered, he was brought to the *Monowitzplatz* the next Sunday morning to be hanged. As we watched.

————

That little bit of medical history and SS "justice" aside, the civilian masters (German engineers) at I.G. Farben Industries did not allow random *SS* or *Kapo* assaults on prisoners during working hours. We were being trained, both on the job and in classrooms, to perform skilled tasks, which gave our lives a certain commercial value beyond those of the instantly disposable construction crews that had built their factories. Of course, when our shifts were finished and we returned to our blocks at Monowitz, we were, as usual, at the mercy of the beasts. We were, after all, *slaves*, and it would not have done for anyone to allow us to forget this. However, relative to Birkenau, we had reasonably decent accommodation — smaller barracks-blocks, single bunks, showers, laundry facilities even. And slit trenches in which to shelter during Allied air raids. (The *SS* and civilian workers had bunkers.) More important, the soup was thicker, the bread ration was 300 grams as opposed to 150, no *Blockältester* or *Schreiberdienst* stole our few grams of margarine, and we received a daily slice of *Blutwurst* (blood sausage made from diced pork fat, pork blood, onions and spices). Friday we got a double ration. All of which meant that in practice, we were treated as "almost human." It was a welcome new experience.

One of the first jobs I had at Monowitz was working three days a week for the *SS* dog master. This veteran of the Eastern Front made it a practice to share his breakfast with me. I am not suggesting that we sat down and ate together. We didn't. Indeed, he never spoke to me, except to give me orders. But out of the kindness of his heart, he would break his morning portion of German rye bread (spread with margarine and marmalade) in half, wrap it in a paper, place it behind a tree, then gesture that I should help myself. Half for him and half for me. The first time this happened, I couldn't believe my eyes. I mean, what does one say about a man like that? He belonged to the same *SS-Totenkopfverbände* responsible for the mass murder of Jews a few kilometres up the road, but his only interests were in breeding and training good strong German Shepherds.

My job was to clean their kennels, and dispose of those puppies that were either deformed at birth or failed to pass the test for aggression at two or three weeks. The dog master would put these in a box, and I would take them outside the kennel area, knock them over the head, and bury them. Not a pleasant job, but it was not onerous. Neither was it particularly shocking to someone raised in the *shtetl,* where domestic animals were slaughtered every day. And as long as I snapped to and made the extra effort at whatever I was doing, my *SS* boss was happy. He didn't even mind when I ate the bits of dog biscuit that his animals left behind (highly nutritious stuff, if you've never tried it). Of course, I was conscious of the fact that the German Shepherds that tracked the unfortunate Polish escapee that I mentioned earlier (and many like him) were bred and trained by this same *SS* dog master. But none of this had anything to do with me. So far as the Nazis are concerned, their evil was and is exclusively their own.

––––––

Several months later in Buna, I had occasion to work for another veteran of the Eastern Front. He too gave me extra pieces of bread. The difference was that this time my German master was *Wehrmacht,* not *SS,* and Communistically inclined. I know the latter to be true because he spent a great deal of time talking to me. He was a technical sergeant, I think. (The *SS* and the *Wehrmacht* did not have the same rank structures.) At any rate, he was a first class electrician. I was under his command and did whatever I was told, which was mainly working in one of the I.G. Farben machine shops making little hot plates that he in turn sold on the black market to other German soldiers.

I didn't care. Why would I? My interest was in staying alive, not helping the German war machine. And I was happy to work hard for him, which was why he came to trust me. I remember him saying, "Germany, ach! It's a useless war. We have no business to be in it." Of course, he knew I wasn't going to tell anybody when he said things like, "There's not going to be any peace treaty. The Allies are going to beat the hell out of us until we give in. Who is going to make peace with Hitler, the son of a bitch." All of which made me nervous. He was far too open. I thought that if I agreed with him, he might report me to the SS. So I kept my mouth shut. He, however, was so genuinely upset about the certain ruination, of his homeland that he never seemed to notice. This was a situation as surprising to me as the virulent anti-Semitism I encountered when I worked briefly for the officer in charge of a group of British prisoners of war. (They must have been prisoners of war, because they had Red Cross food parcels.) In any event, one day, this Englishman, who with his dark curly hair was himself handsome enough to be a Jew, drew his finger across my throat when I took too long to complete a task, and spat out these words, in very bad German I might add, "You're going to die, you goddamned Jew." If I could find that *Wehrmacht* Sergeant today, I would kiss his hands. I didn't fully appreciate this at the time, but he was my friend. My problem was that I didn't know that Germans like him existed. Whereas, if I met that British Nazi s.o.b. with his mirror-shine boots again...

———

For some reason, it came as a shocking revelation that the English also could hate me just for being a Jew. This was a nation in which we had placed such hope when they stood up against Hitler in 1939. And now in 1944, in our hearts we cheered every time a British Lancaster bomber or an American Flying Fortress on a night raid overhead dropped its load of bombs and took out one of our power plants. That they might have dropped their bombs directly on us didn't matter. The closest I came to getting killed was when I was out on one of those diversionary fire-lighting *Kommandos* and some of the German ack-ack, which was intense, came back to earth around me. Blew one of my colleagues to pieces. I remember his arm flying past my head.

I've never heard a satisfactory explanation of why these bombs were not dropped on the rail lines that were still transporting hundreds of thousands of Jews to their deaths, or on the Birkenau gas chambers and crematorium ovens. God knows, it would have been hard for any half-way competent pilot to miss those fiery chimneys! Still, although we fully expected to be liberated by the Russians, we were overjoyed when we heard from some of the civilian workers that the Allies had landed in Normandy.

I came in contact with only a small fraction of the ten or fifteen thousand people who lived and worked in Buna (the I.G. Farben factories covered acres of land). I suppose the most famous of the Buna inmates, whom I occasionally saw at a distance in consultation with some of the civilian masters, was Primo Levi, who later became one of the great Holocaust educators. The fact that he was Italian and already a graduate in chemistry and that I was Polish and a lowly electrical apprentice would not have been an impediment to our association had we worked in the same *Kommando* or lived in the same barracks-block. "Extermination through labour," the *SS* policy for its Buna slaves, was a social equalizer second only to the actual "selection" process in Birkenau. I was a friendly kid. A natural networker. A hustler, who was always looking to make connections. I stayed the hell away from camp entertainments (orchestra concerts, that sort of thing), but I talked to everyone. And I continued to preach my message of hope to every Jew that I met. Of course I was quick to seek out the active members of the Communist party. This was important. Half the cooks in Buna were Communists, and a constant source of extra food.

Buna-Werke I. G. Farbenindustrie K.L. Auschwitz III.

So was the German inmate (he'd been sentenced to five years for fraud) who ran the Monowitz canteen, where those prisoners with money (gentiles of various nationalities) could purchase cigarettes, soap, shoe polish, note paper, and things like that. Hans gave me the job of cleaning up his little (ten-foot-by-ten-foot) shop each evening. Paid me with his daily litre of soup. The best stuff, with big pieces of meat in it. He preferred to feed himself from the food parcels he received from his relatives back home, and from his Buna black market operation. Hans also gave me the occasional cup of *real* coffee, and any damaged cigarettes that he didn't think he could sell.

There were always people prepared to barter their last piece of bread for a smoke. Or rob you for a cigarette if they had nothing to trade. I countered the latter by sharing the surpluses from my trading activities with my friends. Consequently, I always had bodyguards around me. The most important thing of all so far as my ultimate survival was concerned, however, was that I stopped losing weight. At maybe ninety-five pounds, I may have even gained a pound or two before we were transferred to Germany at year-end.

I could not even begin to talk in terms of ultimate survival had it not been for my gradual change of identity from Polish Jew to Russian gentile. From Mendel to Misha. During my last few months at Buna, I worked fabricating electrical parts with four or five Russians. Red Army officers, the ranking member of whom was a Colonel, who had to be forty, forty-five, roughly three times my age. I think largely because I spoke perfect Russian, but also because I was intellectually alive, a go-getter, and the son of St. Petersburg Lancer hero Chaim Mielnicki, about whom I boasted, they began to include me in their society. As an equal. Like my father, they were big, tough, thoroughly decent, and generous men. They were also fantastic organizers. They'd set up a custom manufacturing organization, and were stealing I.G. Farben and the SS blind. They took payment in food. And as I became an integral part of their mob, we began to share what we variously purloined. Once they did a deal with one of I.G. Farben's Polish employees for a broiled chicken. Cut-up. (Obviously, anything you smuggled past the SS guards at the Buna gates had to be packaged in such a way that it could be hidden on your body.) I forget what they custom-machined for this Pole, but I remember my excitement as we gathered to share this "feast" in what my Russian friends had turned into a private area at the back of our shop. I hadn't eaten chicken in three and a half years. Nor they. But when we chewed on it, we couldn't swallow. It had become as pieces of cotton in our mouths. And we had to spit it out. It was cat. (I think the only way you can actually eat cat is stewed, or sliced thin in the Chinese way and wokked.)

I felt at home in the company of these Russian soldiers. They fit the pattern of the men in my father's tales about his comrades in the 1st St. Petersburg Lancers, in terms of their directness, their sense of sharing, their sentimentality. (Given our circumstances, I never did experience the vodka-induced moroseness that my father sometimes talked about — although these guys threatened often enough to drink the blue methanol that Buna produced.) It didn't seem to matter that half the time I didn't know what my new friends were talking about when they were discussing the ins and outs of Soviet politics and military strategy, which they did for hours on end. When I asked a question, however naive, about, say, Stalin or Molotov's thinking when they did their deal with Hitler and Ribbentrop in 1939, they gave me full value for my interest, and more information than I could absorb in reply. What is more, they spent a lot of time telling me about different things that they'd seen or experienced in the Soviet Union, and thus exposed me to a reality that was far different from my schoolboy impressions. This began my transition away from being an ardent Communist. And somewhere in this process, my name got changed to Misha.

The final step in the transformation of my identity came when we began our journey into the smouldering remains of Hitler's "thousand year" Reich in December 1944. We'd been expecting the arrival of the Soviet forces for weeks. They were only a hundred or so kilometres away. But there they stayed, as September turned into October, into November, and finally December. "Where are they?" I kept asking. "Why doesn't Stalin give the order to advance? Don't they know what's going on here?" We had no appreciation of this, of course, but it appears that "Uncle Joe" was content to sit and watch as Hitler eliminated yet another potential problem for him. There would be no Jews left in Central and Eastern Europe to protest Soviet rule.

In any event, we were caught completely by surprise one evening, when our *Blockältester* at the Monowitz camp ordered us to get ready to move out the next morning. This was not an invitation. The SS had not deserted their posts. We might lament our fate, but we could not refuse, or escape. There was no question that I would travel with my Red Army colleagues. They assumed it, and so did I. This, however, was where my Communist connections really paid off. Misha, "the kid," was able to organize six two-kilo loaves of black bread, one for each of us, from his kitchen Party comrades to supplement the small ration we were provided. Reciprocity at its finest. Before we left, they convinced me to remove from my coat the yellow patch that marked me as a Jew. I could pass as a Russian; they would guarantee it. There was nothing about the tattoo on my arm that was different from theirs (my screams at the time it was forcibly needled into my arm caused the inmate charged with this task to abandon any further identification). As to my circumcision, and the possibility of some SS seeing this final proof of my Jewishness, they would never let me shower without their bodies surrounding mine. Besides, if somehow the question did arise, they would attest that I'd had my foreskin removed for medical reasons while in the Red Army. They didn't ask me to abandon my faith. They didn't give a damn about religion. I would travel in their midst: Misha Mielnicki, just another Russian prisoner of war. My father would have approved.

CHAPTER IV

SURVIVOR

Well may the reader ask, "Did the sun never shine in Birkenau and Buna? In the entire two years of your experience there, were the skies never blue?" In answer: "No. Not ever." We had journeyed onto a metaphysical plane of darkness, where the haze of death obscured the heavens. Here the sun was always black. As was such inmate humour as existed. Standing on parade to witness yet another ritual *SS* hanging on the *Platz*, one or other of my comrades might whisper to me, "Hey, Mendel, the guy on the right's from our block. Want to split his bread ration tonight? Ha, ha." Talk about the "banality of evil," to use Hannah Arendt's famous phrase. It was a case of "Ho-hum, there swings another one." The Nazis had created a subterranean world at Auschwitz that was inhabited by scurrying, craven little beings like myself, and ruled by diabolic, troll-like creatures beyond the imagination of even a Tolkien.

As Himmler's slaves, we lived our lives at a level so primitive that the reader's imagination is undoubtedly strained in trying to come to grips with such a reality. For example, when the physical event called sunshine did occur in Birkenau or Buna, I jumped at any chance to stand or sit in it. If I could find a place away from the ever-prying eyes of killer guards and murderous *Kapos*, that is. My mother had taught me well. I knew that if I didn't want my teeth to fall out, I needed vitamin D. The *SS* did not exactly include cod liver oil in our daily rations. Nor, for that matter, did they give us tooth brushes. You cleaned your teeth with your dirty finger nails, or slivers of wood, or by sucking and blowing air and spit through them (the Russian version of dental floss, so my brother Aleksei informed me when I finally met him again in 1992). And you rubbed your gums with your fingers in hopes that this might prevent pyorrhoea. Among the many last things you wanted on earth, this side of being gassed and burned, was to lose your teeth, and thus your ability to trim your broken toe and finger nails.

And because the Grim Reaper was our constant companion in the death camps, we prisoners tended to run each waking hour on pure adrenaline. Which is more than most human bodies or psyches can endure. Studies show that most of those who did survive, like many combat veterans, continue to suffer from post-traumatic stress disorder as a result. But unlike sailors, soldiers or airmen, we had no guns with which to fight. Consequently, survivors have few tales of personal derring-do to share. Just those of unremitting horror. And terror.

Still, I wasn't at all happy when I was forced to leave the principal burial ground of European Jewry. Everything in life is relative. In Pruzany, I was better off than I'd been in Bialystok. In Buna, I was better off than I'd been in Birkenau. My teeth may have been a little loose, and my hairline prematurely receding, but I worked inside where I was warm and dry. I had enough to eat, a sleeping-shelf of my own, and I was subject to the capricious brutality of the *SS* and their inmate henchmen for only half of every day. Most important, I now had survived the Nazis for three and a half years, and liberation by the Red Army seemed at hand. Depending on transportation,

I could be home in Wasilkow in a couple of days. Reunited with my brother and sister. A hero to my friends and neighbours. Or so I fantasized.

I was in a state of depression when we were marched out the gates of Monowitz that cold and sleety morning in December 1944. I didn't know where we were going, or what the future might hold. How many were we? A thousand? Two thousand? Three? I have no clear sense of our numbers, except that as we tramped westward through the slush, our ranks of five stretched as far as my eye could see. This wasn't meant to be a death march, *per se*. The Nazis, we were to discover, had a specific destination in mind, at least for some of us. And a need of our technical skills. But you could never have proved any of this by the way we were treated en route.

For three days, maybe longer, we were forced marched from first light until last. At night, we slept where we stopped. I remember that on one occasion, my friends and I were among those fortunate enough to share the floor of a barn. The other nights, we slept huddled together on the ice and snow in roadside fields. If you began to weaken and started to lag behind, poof, a "kindly" *SS* guard would shoot you in the back of the head. If you had trouble getting up in the morning, the same "instant relief" was provided for your pain. Or one of these *SS* — (What do you call them when you've used up all the synonyms for "evil sons of bitches?" It is said that you can't use terms that are overly crude because this demonstrates an absence of vocabulary. But the fact of the matter is that the English language, reputedly the richest in the world with over a million words, is inadequate in any extended story when it comes to horror, terror, or those who suffer or perpetrate these.) Or one of these evil *SS-sons-of-bitches* would shoot you for the hell of it. Or, more particularly, because your yellow triangle identified you as a Jew.

Surrounded — and sometimes physically supported — by one or other of my Red Army companions, I kept the required pace (albeit most often marching half-asleep, half-awake). And when, finally, we were herded into empty, open coal cars a hundred and fifty or so kilometres distant from Buna, I shared the space these hardened veterans of the Eastern Front commanded, into which no one outside our company dared intrude. I can't tell you how long we were on that train. It was more than a week. But was it two? I don't know. Distance was no measure, because I don't know how circuitous our route was. Certainly, our train had no priority on the tracks. I know that we were without bread for six or seven days. I found myself amazed that one could go this long without food. My friends and I fashioned a sling from our belts, and sustained life by eating the soot-covered snow we scooped up from the rail embankments as the train chugged along. I know that thirty of the hundred or so prisoners packed into our coal car died before we reached our destination. My companions threw their bodies over the side to make more room for the rest of us — something that had to be done at night, because SS rules forbade such action. But I think that we all might have perished had our trip lasted another day or two.

On whatever date it was, possibly the New Year of 1945, our ancient steam locomotive pulled its cars of human cargo to a stop at Mittelbau-Dora, a sub-camp of the Nordhausen concentration camp, near the city of Weimar in central Germany, some seven hundred kilometres from Buna. We were at the site of one of the most important war-industry complexes left in the crumbling, Hitlerian Reich. Mittelbau-Dora supplied slave labour to the vast Mittelwerk underground factories that manufactured and repaired V-1 and V-2 rockets, as well as Messerschmitt engines.

From June 1944 until March 1945, the Nazis fired some 8,000 of the small, jet-propelled V-1s at Britain. Buzz-bombs. And between September and March, more than 1,000 of the far more deadly, liquid-fuelled, ballistic V-2s. These were Hitler's last desperate surprises (his *Vergeltungswaffen* or revenge weapons), as the Allies advanced from Normandy and the Soviets closed in from the North and East. But the fact is that more than twice as many slave labourers died (some 20,000 in all) in digging the tunnels in which to produce this new-age weaponry than were Britons felled under its barrage. And thousands more perished working above ground loading the rockets, where they were subject to the devastation wrought by Allied air raids.

Speaking only for myself, I was grateful to be hustled into the Dora prisoner induction centre to be deloused, showered, head-and-body-shaved, issued a clean striped uniform, assigned a new number (to be displayed on our jackets and pants), and, most of all, to be fed hot, thick, rich soup. In the final analysis, life is better than death. Even when you find yourself forced to wash with a bar of soap that carries the initials "RJF" ("*Rein Juden Fett*"), indicating that the soap had been made from "Pure Jewish Fat!" Without getting into the current debate about whether the *SS* actually made lampshades from the stretched, tanned, and decorated skin of dead Jews or soap from their body fat, a fellow prisoner at Birkenau told me that he had witnessed human bodies being boiled in large cauldrons or vats. Besides, unless this was just another means of ferreting out any undiscovered Jews (our religious laws dictated that we seek out a rabbi to bury these human remains, not clean ourselves with them), why would the *SS* so mark their soap?

A V-2 rocket.

Of course, survival was measured in food. It was, among other things, our principal topic of conversation. Even more so than sex, or money, or cars. Or even news of the War. I doubt there is a survivor alive today who is not preoccupied in some substantial degree with questions related to food and nutrition. More than fifty years after the Holocaust, I still find myself at once astounded and offended when I see anyone throwing away anything edible. Pity the children of survivors: as parents, we never stopped carping at them about eating every scrap on their plates at meal-times, or lecturing them about the nutritional importance of balanced diets. At Dora, at least in the beginning, the food was good, and plentiful. Nearly 700 calories a day: enough to stay alive. The message the civilian management intended to convey was that this was not a "death" camp. Unfortunately, no one told the *SS*.

Somehow, our *SS* masters expected that we would instantly recover from the travail of our journey. And we did. After a good night's sleep in a relatively decent, warm, single-level, wooden barracks (I remember there was straw on the floor), I began classes on how to weld and solder. I do not know the degree to which this is significant, but there were no identifiable Jews, either in my morning welding classes or in the Zawatsky-*Kommando* (to this day, I don't know why they called it that) that occupied the after-noon portion of my twelve-hour shift. As a "nominal" Russian, I slaved underground on one of the assembly lines, where every nationality (Italians, French, Belgians, English, to name a few), except Jews, seemed to be represented. But where death was meted freely nonetheless by our *SS* guards — in the interests of main-taining critical production quotas and standards, no doubt. Of course, there was some actual sabotage (especially by the Russian workers). But if one of the rest of us made an inadvertent error or nodded off during our twelve-hour shifts (we would chatter con-stantly when the guards were not present or even pinch each other to stay awake), we too were subject to summary execution by slow strangulation. An absolutely horrible fate, by *any* standard.

Every day, as we came into work, we were greeted by 10 or 20 new *SS* murder victims dangling from the electrically controlled bars of the overhead cranes that moved the rockets through their various production stages. They looked like a collection of crippled marionettes, with their feet tied together, hands bound behind their backs, swinging in unison as wire death-collars crushed their windpipes. It normally took these prisoners at least thirty minutes to choke to death. And the pieces of wood firmly fastened between their teeth to prevent any last defiant cries of "Fuck Hitler," or "Long live Stalin," increased their torture by stopping their tongues from falling out. Only two or three might actually be conscious, their eyes bulging, as we passed. But any one movement on those lines caused every body, living or dead, to sway in unison. This was the SS's way of reminding us to be "ever vigilant" on the job. The whole thing was so macabre that even the guards tired of this sport after a while. On a number of occasions I observed some SS-Rottenführer or Unterscharführer put some tortured soul out of his misery by giving his legs a hard pull.

At Mittelbau-Dora, as opposed to Buna, the civilian masters (engineers, technicians, tradesmen) made no effort that I could see to keep the SS out of the workplace. Neither did the Wehrmacht, even though this was a defence-production establishment. After I graduated from my soldering and welding course (I had to pass an exacting examination to do so), I spent some time on the line, where, hour after monotonous hour, I joined small aluminum parts to smaller duraluminum parts with my torch. Very precisely. I was among the lowliest of the low, but even I was aware of the ever increasing pressure our masters were under somehow to save Germany from its just desserts. Indeed, their fear of failure was palpable. I can't imagine that these people were subject to SS reprisals, but I witnessed master after German master, who, instead of accepting responsibility when he made a mistake, pointed his finger at some unfortunate and entirely innocent slave-labourer.

The way this worked was that the masters would take their complaints to the civilian plant manager, Arthur Rudolf, who in turn would report the alleged miscreants to the SS, which made these German civilians as guilty of murder as the black-shirted killers who so joyed in their profession. In my opinion, Arthur

A captured V-2 rocket, still in production.

Rudolf, Wernher von Braun, the overall rocket project director, and their colleagues should have been tried at Nuremberg for their crimes against humanity along with all the other German war criminals. That the United States deemed these "scientists" too valuable for such justice has never impressed me. Nor have the "contributions" of Rudolf, von Braun, and their Nazi buddies to the American defence and space programs made me change my mind. These criminals lived out their lives in luxury and undeserved honour. I felt physically ill when US President Jimmy Carter marked the occasion of von Braun's death in 1977, by declaring, "All the people of the world have profited from his work."

I find it difficult to forget that a few weeks before my eighteenth birthday I was sentenced to death at Mittelbau-Dora. This would have been in mid or late February 1945, just before I finished my welding classes. These had taken place every morning between six a.m. and noon. The rest of the day I was assigned to the general labour Zawatsky-*Kommando*, delivering material in a little metal wagon to the production lines that produced the forty-seven-foot, 13.5 ton V-2 missiles. Anyway, I'd made a connection with one of the cooks, a fellow Communist, who was prepared to give me extra soup after my shift ended, if I had something in which to carry it away. The fact is that I didn't need this additional ration. As I mentioned, we were well enough fed at Dora. But I wanted to have something that I could share with my Russian comrades.

So, one Monday or Tuesday during our half-hour lunch break, I went back into the shop to make a mess tin out of a piece of scrap aluminum that I retrieved from the recycling bin. This was a ten-minute job at most, and I'd just about finished when I heard the unmistakable sound of jackboots coming up behind me. They belonged to an *SS-Unterscharführer* (the same as Kuhnemann). He obviously knew that I shouldn't have been in there by myself, and he wanted to know what the hell I thought I was doing. I couldn't very well tell him that I was making a nose cone for a V-2 rocket, so I told him the truth. More or less. That I was making a container out of a piece of discarded metal so that I could *beg* any leftover soup from the camp kitchen. (You were honour-bound never to reveal any of your accomplices.)

Whereupon this sergeant took off his big black greatcoat belt and beat me across the back and shoulders with it. Didn't touch my face. That was against the "rules." He then wrote down my number, confiscated my mess tin, and marched away. And that was the end of that, or so I thought. I hadn't fouled a rocket assembly, so I knew that I wasn't going to be strangled on the wires. I considered that I'd got off lucky. He could have hit me with a piece of metal and broken some of my bones. But when we assembled for roll call at six p.m., my number was called out. I was taken before the *SS* officer of the day, where I was formally charged with sabotage in the theft of property belonging to the Third Reich, found guilty, and sentenced to be hanged the following Sunday at *Appellplatz*.

I spent the rest of the week inside the *SS* bunker in a four-by-six-foot cage in which I couldn't stand upright, and where I was fed a little bread and half a litre of soup once a day, and was provided a bucket for such waste as this produced. The strange thing is that my mind has blotted out any memory of the despair

I must have felt. I know that I profoundly regretted making that damned mess tin. Had I known that taking a piece of scrap was a capital crime, I wouldn't have done it. There were endless ways to get yourself murdered by the *SS*, and I'd been a witness to most of them. I thought I knew the ropes, and I must have cursed my stupidity. What was I doing getting myself hanged at this late stage in my career as a prisoner? The Germans were losing the War. Liberation might be any day. Did I pray? Probably. Did I wail? Possibly. Most likely, if my cell was warm, I slept a lot. Or maybe I worried about the horrendous boil that was coming to a head on my inner right thigh. Contrary to conventional wisdom, and to the redoubtable Dr. Johnson of course, I don't think that the prospect of being hanged in a few days wonderfully concentrates the mind at all.

Luckier than lucky: what I hadn't dared even to dream of happened at the eleventh hour. A general amnesty for the prisoners on Dora's death row. I don't know the reason for this. At the time, I thought the Germans had won a victory somewhere, but I can find no record of any Nazi military success in February 1945, unless it was in momentarily delaying the Soviet capture of Berlin. Frankly, I don't need to know the reason. It is sufficient that I am alive, and not a long-forgotten corpse. My luck, however, had a price. My sentence was commuted to 25 lashes. At the Dora *Appellplatz* on the Sunday originally scheduled for my execution, after I was judged physically fit by an *SS* doctor, I was bent over a table and my hands and feet secured into a stock-like affair, with my skinny bare ass at a height convenient to the muscular Nazi assigned to administer my punishment. (In the circumstances, no one noticed either my boil or my missing foreskin, both reasons for execution in themselves.)

I cannot describe the pain that this young *SS* inflicted with his leather-covered, wooden (possibly metal — I never did get a good look at it, but it was stiff) three-inch-wide paddle. Had I been capable of thought, and given the choice, I think I would have opted for the gallows. Fortunately, all my circuits shut off after the first four or five mind-searing thwacks. The next thing I knew, someone was pouring a bucket of ice-cold water over my head to revive me. Released from the stocks, I had to "fall in" (take my accustomed place in the ranks of those assembled) to watch the rest of that morning's "ritual entertainment." The skin and muscles of my now deep-purple and black buttocks had tightened to such a degree that I could barely walk. I shuffled, stiff-legged and sideways, like some malfunctioning robot. Thank God, there was no blood. Had that *SS* guard cut me with the edge of his paddle, which he easily could have done, I would not have recovered. Gangrene would have set in, as it would have had the flesh on my bottom separated from the bone. Where on the list of human horrors does one place the prospect of having that precious part of one's anatomy rot away? As it was, the numbness quickly gave way to a brutal, cruel, and ruthless throbbing. A circle of agony about seven inches in diameter across the two cheeks of my ass. I couldn't bear to touch it even with a finger. Tears blinded me as I stood there on the *Platz*. I was a mess.

I think it fair to say that at this point I began slowly to lose my mind. I have only fragments of memory of my final two months of captivity. I do know that my Russian comrades treated me like a very special person, a hero, as I slowly recovered from my ordeal over the next three weeks. And that they continued to protect my identity, in the showers and elsewhere at Dora. As I say, I recall little about any of this, but I have the impression of everyone being nice to me. The German welding master shared some bread with me, which was very kind because rations had started to get short for everyone. (I think the flour they were using was now fifty percent sawdust.) The *Kapos*, who were entirely German criminal inmates, took care not to give me jobs that would aggravate my condition. For example, when I was assigned my place on the assembly line, I was never required to sit. Which was wonderful, because I remember being afraid that I might be shot or strangled if I couldn't do my work properly. And one of the Nazi officers broke the rules (it was forbidden to take anyone to hospital for the treatment of a punishment) to give me some salve to soften the skin over my bruises. Why? The Russians looked after me because they accepted me as one of their own. But the Germans? Maybe they finally realized that the War was over, and that "we Russians" would soon be in a position to take revenge. I don't know. What I do know is that the milk of ethnic and religious tolerance had not begun suddenly to course through their veins, and that they would have pushed me over the edge had they even suspected that I was a Jew.

In this connection, I must recount an event that took place a week or so before my being sentenced to death. We were still receiving our full bread ration after roll call in the evenings. My practice was to eat half, and save half for the morning. The question was how to keep this staff of life safe overnight. My solution was to roll my trousers carefully around it (thus protecting both my breakfast and my appearance), and place this bundle under my head as a pillow. Well, very early one morning, I was awakened when my head hit the wooden sleeping shelf beneath it with a thud. I knew instantly what had happened. I was out of my bunk and onto the back of the prisoner who'd stolen my bread in a second. But not fast enough to stop him from stuffing my bread into his mouth. Possessed of a strength that in retrospect still surprises me, I quickly had him down on the floor with my hands locked on his throat, when the Polish priest, who was our *Blockältester*, came out of his room to see who was making all the racket.

I can't say whether it was my intention to strangle the thief or just to stop him from swallowing my bread (and thus my ability to stay alive). Whatever the case, I was on the brink of choking the final breath out of the man, when this priest, who was tall, and heavy enough to have pulled me away with one hand, instead said, "So what will you accomplish if you kill him? He's already eaten most of your bread, and you'll be hanged tomorrow. Remember your Ten Commandments. Let him go, and I'll tend to his punishment." So I let the son of a bitch go. At which point the big priest added, "God will help you." In Hebrew! Somehow, he had known from the outset that I was a Jew. I don't recall that in my subsequent dealings with him, which, given his position, were considerable, he ever so much as alluded to this again. And I couldn't be more grateful to this Christian man of the cloth if I tried. In his own way, he too saved my life.

However, if I truly owe my continued presence on this earth to anyone, it is to Sasha, one of my Russian comrades. I don't know if the Colonel had assigned him the specific task of minding me after my public beating by the SS, or if this occurred after we were transferred to Bergen-Belsen. I have no recollection at all of our leaving Mittelbau-Dora after production at the Mittelwerk factories was shut down sometime in mid to late March. All I know is that we went by train. That the journey seemed short. That, on our arrival, we were crammed, sometimes ten to a single sleeping shelf, into barracks unfit for pigs. That we had no work or other activity, apart from being counted and beaten by ethnic SS guards. That our rations were pitiful, even by Birkenau standards (27,000 male and female prisoners died of disease or starvation in March alone, among them a fifteen-year-old girl by the name of Anne Frank). And that we were literally, quite literally, starved from 8 or 9 April until our liberation on 15 April. That is to say, for an entire week, we were denied access to all food and water by the machine guns of the Hungarian, Bosnian Moslem, and Croatian SS guards who continued to man the camp watchtowers, even after Kommandant Kramer and the majority of the German SS officers had fled.

When the British Army arrived, I lay at death's door, a human bag of bones (although, curiously, one with swollen feet and ankles), too weak at seventy pounds to move much more than my cracked lips. I remember that there was shit everywhere. All over the floor. Dripping down from the bunks. And dead bodies beyond the scope of any normal person's imagination. I was

Joseph Kramer, Kommandant of Bergen–Belsen concentration camp.

surrounded, in and outside my block, by ten thousand decaying corpses. People in my block were using them for pillows. And one of us was adding to their number on the average of every two to three minutes. And, as the reader might imagine, there were *billions* of lice. Death and disease were so rampant that for the last two weeks the *SS* guards refused to enter our blocks. (Probably, many have seen the *unedited* film footage of Bergen-Belsen that the British government belatedly released in 1995. If not, they should.)

Sasha was in his mid-thirties, a Captain or a Major in the Red Army, a scientist, and a very educated man. In Bergen-Belsen, he risked his life to save us. The *SS* had plans to kill every last prisoner, male and female. They'd allowed the wells to be fouled, thus denying us water. Then, as I said, they stopped our already meagre rations. In the meantime, or so I later heard, they built up a supply of thousands of loaves of bread. Each one injected with cyanide. They calculated that we'd be so desperate for food that we'd never notice. And probably we wouldn't have. For some reason, this Nazi *coup de grâce* was not effected. Not that we knew any more than that we were dying of hunger.

About two or three days into our famine, Sasha, on a midnight foray around the camp, managed to break into the root cellar next to the *SS* cookhouse. Dodging bullets from the *SS* machine guns, he made it back to our block with several potatoes, but minus half of his left ear. By this time, I was in and out of consciousness. But it seemed that every time I opened my eyes, there was Sasha, his head bandaged with the sleeve of my shirt, patiently placing a wafer-thin, moist strip from one of these potatoes (cut with the rusty lid from a tin can) into my mouth, which was as much as I could manage to chew and swallow at a time. This is the only reason I was still alive when the British finally arrived. If I could find Sasha today, I would kiss his hands and feet.

I suspect that I heard about our liberation on 15 April. I don't remember. I do know that when the British finally got themselves organized a couple of days later, Sasha and the Colonel carried me outside so that I could receive the medical attention I required. I can only believe that they insisted upon it. Certainly, I was in no condition to do so. Let me be frank: I *survived* liberation by the British; thirteen thousand of my fellow prisoners in Bergen-Belsen didn't. And I don't think the British war cabinet or high command could have cared less. We were a nuisance, an inconvenience, a drain on their resources. They had three weeks of war to complete, geopolitical goals to achieve, and we were an unexpected impediment to their progress. When I was well enough to understand what was going on, I wasn't very happy about the way they treated us.

I still think they could have saved many, if not most of the people who were dying in extreme misery from dysentery and typhus. (Compare, if you like, what the Swedish medical team was

Liberation.

able to achieve in the women's camp at Bergen-Belsen with the paltry British effort in the men's.) I further believe that they bull-dozed thousands of our dead into mass graves to prevent disease from spreading to the German civilian population. My God, initially, they left the Hungarian *SS* guards in their watchtowers to prevent us from leaving that hellhole. And fed them better than they fed us. This was for our own good they said. In fact, the British cared so much about our protection that, after our "liberation," a German Stuka was able to dive down and machine-gun our barracks without fear of return fire. I don't know anyone who doesn't wish that he or she had been liberated by the Soviets or the Americans.

A Bergen–Belsen mass grave.

For over fifty years, I've heard every excuse the British and their apologists could invent, and none of them impresses me. After all we'd been through at the hands of the Nazis, we deserved a great deal better. As to Winston Churchill's agreement to Stalin's demand that all Russian prisoners of war be forcibly repatriated to the Soviet Union, I am speechless at the thought of what must certainly have happened to Sasha, the Colonel, and my other Red Army comrades as a result. To be shot as traitors on their return, or to be condemned for the rest of their lives to the horrors of the Gulag for surrendering to the Germans after their armies had been defeated at Minsk in 1941 was a fate these heroes did not deserve.

To me, the most impressive figure (apart from my Russians of course) in our liberation from Bergen-Belsen was a camp physician by the name, I seem to recall, of Kurtzky. Initially, I thought him *SS* — but now I think he must have been *Wehrmacht*. Whatever the case, I remember this German-speaking gentile saying, "As long as there is one Jewish prisoner sick here, I'm going to stay." And stay he did. He organized a clinic from among the local doctors to supplement the medical services provided by the British, and worked day and night to save the sick and dying. I met him many times after I recovered. In fact, when I was well enough physically (which amazingly took only a couple of weeks), I became a member of the ten-man, prisoner-run, security force that the British eventually created to see that everything worked well, and in the best interests of our fellow survivors, until we were all transferred to Allied recovery and displaced person camps. It was in this context that I came to know Dr. Kurtzky.

Two of us had always to accompany him when he was moving about the camp. Many of our colleagues would have killed the doctor had they been allowed to get their hands on him. It didn't matter that Dr. Kurtzky had had nothing to do with the killings or medical experiments at Bergen-Belsen, and had in fact saved lives. To the majority of my fellow internees a German officer was a German officer, whether *SS* or *Wehrmacht*. The members of our prisoner police force didn't have guns or clubs. We had armbands. We talked people out of committing gratuitous acts of violence, if we could. We also discouraged them from leaving the camp before they were medically fit, lest they gorge themselves on salamis and jams and other rich foods (which often killed them when they did). I suppose some of our fellows thought we were being hypocritical, because we were bunked in the former *SS* officers' barracks, where we had our own cook, and decent, in fact delicious, food — including chickens from the farms in the nearby countryside. For the few weeks that this lasted, Dr. Kurtzky was our guest each Friday for Sabbath dinner. I thought him a fantastic person, and I'm upset that not many people today know his name, or the number of Jewish lives that were saved by his courage and dedication.

———

By the middle of August 1945, I'd been processed. That is to say, declared free of contagious diseases and issued travel documents by the American military administration to return to Poland. There was no psychological counselling, no group therapy sessions, no educational programs. Nothing. We were treated as if the Holocaust had never happened. In my case, as if nearly four years of starvation and terror in the ghettos and the camps, as if the murder of my mother and my father, as if the uncertain fate of my sister and my brother (to say nothing of the probable fate of my uncles, aunts, cousins, and friends), as if the dreams of continuing *SS* pursuit that left me sweating and screaming in the night, as if the termination of my formal education at the age of fourteen by an invading army bent on the murder of my people, were but everyday occurrences in a young man's development. So far as I know, no one in any position of authority on the Allied side paid the slightest attention to the high incidence of suicide among the 250,000 to 300,000 Jewish survivors. In my observation, most of us were on fragile emotional ground. I know I was. I still am. Indeed, everyone who endured the ordeal of living in Birkenau or any other concentration camp, where he or she was condemned to smell the burning flesh of his or her brothers and sisters twenty-four hours a day, should have been treated as a permanently handicapped person.

———

According to the travel papers I received when the British and Americans finally released me from their care and custody, I was

Mendel Mielnicki, eighteen years old, Jewish, a Polish citizen, from Wasilkow, Bialystok Province, Poland. A Displaced Person, or D.P., with yet another number: something I didn't intend to be for long. I was headed *home*. But not, I decided, in the company of the Christian Poles who were being shipped en masse from the Allied sectors of Germany. One look told me that these people were the same old anti-Semites that I'd known all my life. Still, I didn't want to travel by myself. So, when the opportunity presented itself, I joined a small wagon train of young women (both Christian and Jewish) making their way back to Poland and Russia. They thought that the presence of a Russian-speaking male in their midst might be to their advantage. As one of them said to me, "I was never raped by German soldiers, and I don't want to be raped by the Russians." I guess they thought that I posed no danger in that regard. Of course, they were right. A little kissing and cuddling at night with one or other of those who particularly liked you was considered kosher, but unwanted pregnancies or venereal diseases were not high on any of our lists. And I did prove useful in fending off curious, and no doubt horny, Red Army foot soldiers.

Our destination was the German-Polish border near Poznan (Posen). If I recall correctly, we were some thirty people in all. We travelled the back roads in three canvas-topped, hay wagons, each pulled by a team of work horses that had been requisitioned (or perhaps merely "liberated") from some of the nearby German peasants. It was slow going, but the weather was fine. We didn't have any money, but we were able to live off the land in the sense that we simply asked for what we needed en route. When we needed food and no public kitchens were available, we went up to a farmhouse or other dwelling and told the woman in charge (there were hardly ever men present) what we wanted. This applied to clothing, and other items as well. If I said I needed some clean underwear, or trousers, or better boots, invariably the answer was "Take it, take it." Some survivors became quite well off "liberating" the possessions of the now vanquished Germans. Not me. Some clothes, boots, a couple of leather suitcases, and a Leica camera were all I ever "accepted" from our now most gracious hosts. Of course, in their generosity, these Germans also

Michel's D.P. Card.

gave us back the lice the British had so scrupulously eliminated from our bodies.

The only incident worth recording about our two weeks on the road came as the result of a side trip I took into Berlin, which I wanted to see while I had the chance. Rides were easy enough to hitch back and forth, and I was only away from the women for the better part of a day. Anyway, I'd been wandering through the rubble of this once great city for a while when I began to get hungry. I was somewhere around the Brandenburg Gate when I spotted a Russian officer. I went up to him and asked where the public kitchens were. I didn't notice at first, but then I realized this guy was very drunk.

I told him I was a survivor from a concentration camp. He started in about how I spoke such good Russian. I explained that although I was a Polish Jew, my father had been born in Russia, and that I'd attended a Russian-language gymnasium after we'd become part of the Soviet Union in 1939. He asked if I spoke German too, and I said yes. At which point, he pulled out his revolver and put it to my head. "You're a bloody spy!" he said. "To have survived the War as a Jew, you had to have worked for the Germans. I'm going to blow your brains out."

I believed his threat. We'd been travelling through the Soviet Zone for days, and I'd seen Russian soldiers kill people on the street for no apparent reason. I'd also seen them shoot out unbroken German windows with their machine guns just for fun. So I knew that I had to think very fast if I was going to talk him out of this. I said, "Listen, I'm a *witness* to what happened to the Russian officers who were prisoners of war in Poland and Germany. A *witness* to how the Nazis mistreated, starved, and killed them. I'm a *witness* to that. There will be court cases. You gonna kill me? Who is going to talk for those people who were killed if you do?"

At the time, although I knew that the leading Nazis had been arrested by the occupying powers, as had SS officers like Bergen-Belsen *Kommandant* Kramer, I'd never given any thought to whether there were going to be War Crimes Trials or not. Certainly, no British or American officer had ever indicated the slightest interest in recording any of my experiences. My being a "*witness*" was a notion that came into my mind for the first time as I stood there with this drunk's revolver pressing against my forehead. I don't know the extent to which he grasped the full measure of the idea I was expressing, but he put away his gun, and told me to go to hell. I got out of there fast, amazed that I had been able to talk myself out of a situation that tight. I have been a *Holocaust witness* ever since, which has been its own kind of hell.

Before we'd parted company in Birkenau in early 1943, my brother Aleksei and I had vowed to meet at our home in Wasilkow, if we survived the Nazi war against our people. Little did I know that Aleksei, in his rush to keep this promise, had left the Mauthausen concentration camp shortly after its liberation by the Americans without either fully recovering his health or receiving his travel documents. In consequence, when he was apprehended by the Soviets just before he reached Warsaw, he had nothing, save the number 98039 on his left forearm, to prove who he was. Because, like me, he spoke perfect Russian, and now Ukrainian as well (a result of nearly two years working for a Ukrainian *Kapo* on a roof repair *Kommando*), he was judged a Soviet citizen and inducted into the Red Army for a term of compulsory military service. Thus, while I was wending my way towards the Polish border, he was being forced to march a thousand kilometres or more to Kishinev, the capital of Moldavia, to begin his military training.

He was to have his own experience at the hands of drunken Russian officers. Simply because he was a Jew, they attacked him in his bed one night, and brutally beat him, so much so that he was hospitalized for two months with a number of broken bones (including one in his nose that never did heal properly). He'd gone from one form of enslavement to another, with hardly a pause for breath. Because he was never allowed to leave the Soviet Union to search for Lenka or me, he eventually accepted that we hadn't survived, and got on with such life as was permitted a Jew in Stalinist Russia after his release from the army in 1950.

In the meantime, I'd waited for Aleksei in Bialystok (you couldn't actually wait in Jewless Wasilkow anymore, unless you wanted to be murdered) until I thought it reasonable to conclude that he hadn't survived the Nazi murder machine. It was only in late 1946, when I was in Paris, that I met a survivor from Mauthausen who told me that he'd seen my brother alive after the camp's liberation. Then I heard that someone else had heard that he was a conscript in the Red Army's 100th Infantry in Kishinev.

I asked the International Red Cross and various other aid organizations to help me find him. Requests for information were made on my behalf, but the Soviets ignored them. The Iron Curtain was a reality that seemed destined ever to keep Aleksei and me apart.

Brothers reunited after 50 years.

Ironically, it was *SS-Unterscharführer* Heinrich Kuhnemann (or, more particularly, his War Crimes Trial at Duisburg in 1991) who brought us back together after an interregnum of nearly fifty years. At the time, *perestroika* and *glasnost* were the new order in what was still Gorbachev's Russia, and Aleksei had taken the opportunity this had provided to journey to Auschwitz, where he filed a written request for confirmation of his imprisonment there, so that he, at long last, could claim compensation from the German government. Meanwhile, in Vancouver, I had begun to worry about whether some old Nazi or some new neo-Nazi skinhead would attempt to assault or even murder me if I appeared to testify against the criminal Kuhnemann. Unfortunately, as I've grown older, it has become my second nature to fret, and, in consequence, to become clinically depressed (part of my death-camp legacy, it seems); being a dead hero has never been high on my list of personal ambitions. In the event, of course, I knew where my duty lay, and so boarded the plane for Germany in search of justice for my father, my mother, the Jew with the gold pocket watch, my friend Yossele, and all the rest of Kuhnemann's victims.

Naturally, after my wife June and I arrived in Duisburg, I spent a great deal of time in conversation with the German prosecutor in charge of Kuhnemann's case, a fine man by the name of Dr. Feld. Because my story could not be told without reference to Aleksei, the subject of his possible whereabouts was much discussed as well. Dr. Feld didn't consider that Aleksei's testimony would be necessary to convict Kuhnemann, but undertook for my sake to find my brother, if he were still alive. And, some months later, almost by chance during an official visit to Auschwitz, he discovered Aleksei's certification request. This German gentleman then tracked my brother down, with the help of the Russian authorities, with the result that on 15 June 1992 I received official notification from the German Consulate General in Vancouver that a Mr. Aleksej Haimowicz Mielnicki resided at Ul. Straitieley 16/46, Iwano-Frankowsk, Ukraine (the former Polish city of Stanislawow). For four years, until his death in 1996 from a third heart attack, we celebrated our reunion by phone and letter, and in person during an extended visit June and I made to his home in August 1992. To have found one's brother after fifty years was a reward of cosmic proportion, but it would have been sweeter by far if I could have reported to Aleksei that I'd helped send former *SS-Unterscharführer* Heinrich Kuhnemann to prison.

As to Lenka, she didn't even try to return to Wasilkow. After she escaped from the train that was transporting women internees

Lenka.

from Birkenau to their likely deaths in concentration camps in the Nazi fatherland, an older Sudeten-German woman (whose son was a *Wehrmacht* officer) found her wandering in the night, took her in, and kept her hidden from the *SS* for over four months until the German surrender in May 1945. Far quicker than I, she heard about the renewal of anti-Semitic violence in Poland. She knew our mother and father were dead. And, obviously, she thought that Aleksei and I had been murdered as well. So, what was there for her to go back to?

Instead, she made her way to Prague, where she was given refuge by an older, very rich, Jewish doctor and his Christian wife. Prior to the War, Dr. Bohin had been personal physician to the founder-President of the Czechoslovakian Republic, Tomas Masaryk; and, during the War, both a prisoner and head doctor at Theresienstadt. In any event, the Bohins had never had any children, and they liked my sister so much that they wanted to adopt her. It was from Prague that Lenka wrote to our Uncle Isadore in Paterson, New Jersey (which was where she still dreamed of living). When, in late 1945, I moved from Bialystok to Breslau (which had been ceded to Poland at the War's end), I also wrote to Uncle Isadore. Thus did Lenka and I find each other. I was so excited when I received her first letter and the photographs inside that I ran someone down with my motorcycle in my rush to get home to show these to my friends. We were reunited the next spring, and moved to Paris together, where we began our lives anew in a crummy little hotel that had been a brothel before and during the War.

Coming back to my wagon train experience: when finally we reached the border, the Polish Customs guards (maybe they were Army) seized our horses, wagons, and everything else they fancied (they were particularly fond of accordions) as the price of our admission. Mind you, they were without prejudice. They stole your property without regard to nationality or religion. *Welcome home.* Of course, this was all stuff that we had "liberated" from the Germans. It reminded me of my mother's wisdom: "If you steal things, you'll find that you don't get to keep them for very long." (I can only hope that this also applied to these gentile border guards as well.) Still, our rude reception at the border wasn't the end of the earth. Because we all had our American papers, we were allowed to ride the trains in Poland without payment, and public soup kitchens existed to feed us in every community of any size.

At Poznan, my companions and I parted company, some to stay, others to proceed in various directions. At the local soup kitchen, I was encouraged to proceed no further. The city's German population had been expelled. Fully furnished apartments were there for the taking. Gratis. "This is a safe place for Jews," I was told by a city official. "The rest of Poland isn't." This was the first

I'd heard that members of the Polish *AK* (*Armia Krajowa*) or Home Army had formed partisan bands in support of the Polish Government in Exile in London, and to drive any remaining Jews from *their* land. It was incredible to me that, having survived the Nazis, I should now have to worry about being murdered by some local fascist. But that was indeed the case. In the two years following the end of the War, more than 100,000 of Poland's remaining Jews fled the country of their birth in fear for their lives. However, as August turned to September in 1945, there was no question in my mind that I would proceed with all possible speed to Bialystok. And this I did, without incident.

It was only after I reached Bialystok that the racist reality of my homeland began to sink in. I arrived in the middle of the night. The train station, which had been destroyed during a German air raid in September 1939, was as I remembered it. A pile of rubble. The switchman who was on duty saw me standing on the ramp with my suitcases. Three things were immediately obvious to him. One, I was Jewish. Two, no one was meeting me. And three, I had no idea as to where I should go. He came up to me and said, "I wouldn't wander the streets tonight if I were you. At best, you'll be beaten and robbed. At worst, you'll be murdered. There's a wooden bench in my switch-shack [which contained the controls for the railyard], you'd better sleep on that." At first, I worried that maybe this guy wanted to rob me himself, but, lacking an alternative, I followed him down the track. As it turned out, he was just a good Christian man helping out a seriously lost young Jew.

In the morning, I hied myself down to the Jewish community centre. The city had been largely destroyed. It wasn't as bad as Warsaw, but it had been a battleground the previous summer, when the Germans had made a stand against the advancing Soviet forces. Those few Bialystoker Jews who had managed to escape the Nazi roundups began to return after the Red Army liberated what was left of the town on 27 July 1944. Returning concentration

Michel in Bialystok, 11 September 1945.

camp survivors now added to their number. But, at most, we numbered a few hundred out of a permanent pre-War Jewish population of more than 60,000, if one counted both the city and the surrounding districts. It was an experience that lent substance to the horrendous numbers beginning to emerge as journalists and other researchers began the task of calculating the magnitude of the Nazi slaughter.

Of course, the first thing that I did was to check the huge notice board on which all visitors were supposed to post their names and addresses, as well as their destinations if they were moving on. Aleksei and Lenka had yet to arrive. I recognized a few names on the board, but none who were related to me. It was all terribly depressing. Especially when I was advised that a returning

Jew ventured into Wasilkow at his peril. One of the many stories in circulation was about the young newlyweds who had gone to reclaim the groom's family home. The peasants occupying it had made them welcome, fed them dinner, and had volunteered to vacate the premises as soon as possible. As the hour was getting late and public transportation back to Bialystok nonexistent, the couple was invited to spend the night. The next day, their headless corpses were found along the roadside.

Although it was fast becoming obvious that Poland held no future for me, I was still trying to figure out what to do, when, a couple of days after my arrival, I ran into Mrs. Bogucki, the wife of the former manager of the Wasilkow power plant. Her husband (one of my father's Christian friends) had been sent to Siberia by the Soviets for his "economic crimes" after they nationalized all electrical generation facilities in 1939. In turn, Mrs. Bogucki had been driven out of Wasilkow by her Christian neighbours for trying to help some of the town's Jews after the Nazi invasion in 1941. Apparently, they'd branded her a "Jew lover." As a boy, I'd been in her home a number of times in the company of my father — to admire their Christmas lights, among other things. In any event, we recognized each other. I couldn't believe how glad she was to see me. It was like she was my mother.

She insisted that I get my bags from the room I was sharing with, I think, three or four other people, and come home with her. Which I did gladly. Whereupon she poured me a hot bath, presented me with delousing shampoo and a container of delousing powder, and took away all my clothes, which she then boiled to kill the rest of my tiny, parasitic, travelling companions. Afterwards, with me dressed in some of her husband's clothes, she and her son and I talked and talked and talked. I was shocked when I learned what had happened to the Jews of Wasilkow. For their part, they could barely believe my descriptions of Birkenau and Bergen-Belsen.

The next morning, Mrs. Bogucki (who, by the way, now ran

a small, salami-manufacturing operation out of her house) retained a lawyer to act for me. Her daughter had married a local policeman, so the connections were there. Then, we hired her son-in-law's father, who owned a hansom cab (horse and buggy), to take us to visit the people who had taken possession of the Mielnicki house in Wasilkow.

Michel making new friends in Bialystok.

I made it clear to these folks that the house was for sale. If they wanted it, I'd make them a good price. Otherwise, I'd put it on the market. It really wasn't a complicated negotiation. They'd kept the house and property in good condition. The sight of my mother's garden in its September glory brought tears to my eyes. For the equivalent of two hundred American dollars (which, at three thousand to one, was a lot of *zlotys* in 1945), these people had a bargain. What is more, unlike tens, if not hundreds of thousands of other Polish gentiles, they would not be living off the blood of murdered Jews. As an unexpected bonus, I discovered that I also held title to my Uncle Shmulke's house. My cousin Yosel's bastard son had been unsuccessful in his attempt to establish any legal relationship to his father and grandfather. So I sold that as well. At

Michel and friends at the memorial to the Bialystok–area Jews murdered by the Nazis.

the fabulous price of three hundred dollars American to a gentile couple from Bialystok, who wanted a weekend retreat near the Suprasl River.

The problem with all this real estate business was that I'd made myself visible in Wasilkow. And the word spread that Chaim Mielnicki's son was back in town. A week or so later, as I was opening Mrs. Bogucki's front door one late night after attending a party, two bullets whistled past my head. I have no proof of this, but I have always believed this attempt on my life to be the work of some local fascist that the NKVD, on my father's recommendation, had sent to a labour camp in Siberia.

Perhaps I flatter myself to the extent that I would rather have been shot at by Polish racists than by the enraged relatives of Cousin Yosel's common-law wife. I hadn't taken anything away from her kid. He didn't live in Shmulke's house. As he neither physically possessed nor legally owned the property in question, if I hadn't made a dollar on it, no one would have. Whoever my would-be assassin, he caused me to abandon any lingering thoughts of staying in Bialystok.

However, I couldn't leave immediately. Aleksei might show up any day. So might Lenka. Besides, I didn't know where to go. In the meantime, I used some of my new wealth to buy myself two or three decent suits, other apparel, and some good boots and shoes. All of this I purchased secondhand from roadside stalls, which was where I met Mrs. Buchowska, another Christian exile from Wasilkow, who was selling very pricey antique jewellery. She immediately invited me to dinner at what can only be described as her mansion, where I again met her two perfectly gorgeous daughters. I thought I looked pretty swish in my knee-high riding boots and three-piece, grey tweed suit. So apparently did they. What a fuss they made over me. As did a lot of the young women with whom I came in contact.

It was all rather confusing. I lost my virginity in Bialystok. To a gentile girl from Grodno. I wish I could say that the experience was fantastic, but I recall clearly that I wasn't very good, and that she wasn't exactly hygienic. Or very interested in the quality of my performance. Turned out that what she really wanted was for me to repair her boots. The next morning, I did that as well.

Otherwise, I spent a lot of time listening to news and rumours about what was happening in the rest of the country, or talking with the new friends I'd made about what we might do in the future. But after two or three weeks of this, I rather tired of hanging about. Rather tired too of always looking over my shoulder to see if anyone was coming up behind me with a gun. My dreams of a hero's reception had been shattered, and I knew that I had to get out of Bialystok, and as quickly as possible. My continued presence posed a danger not only to my own life, but to that of Mrs. Bogucki as well. From what I'd heard, the commercial opportunities in Breslau, the former capital of Lower Silesia, were enormous. Like Poznan, Breslau had become Polish at the end of the War, and its German population had been expelled. So I decided to try my luck there. Consequently, I put my name and destination on the notice board at the Jewish community centre, and boarded the train south.

Somewhere between Bialystok and Warsaw, Polish *AK* (Home Army) bandits on horseback managed to stop our progress. It was like something out of a wild west movie. With one of their number holding the engineer and fireman at gunpoint, they began searching the passenger cars for Russians and Jews, whom they pulled from their seats and forced off the train. Along with their baggage and other possessions, of course. I don't know if this happened or not, but it seemed to me that they intended to shoot these poor souls.

It was at this point that I decided that if I emerged alive from this renewed assault on my being that I'd get the hell out of Poland as quickly as possible. That as soon as I arrived in Breslau, I'd write to Uncle Isadore to ask him to sponsor my immigration to the United States. I think that my split second decision pricked up my courage to the point that when this AK asshole approached my seat, I ignored him, and continued to read my newspaper (which fortunately was in Polish, not Yiddish). When he poked my paper with the barrel of his machine gun, and demanded: "Are you a Jew?" I sneered in reply: "What? Are you trying to insult me?" "Sorry," he said. Me too, I thought to myself.

EPILOGUE AND AFTERWORD

BY JOHN MUNRO

As Mendel/Misha (soon to be Michel) Mielnicki indicates in his own account, upon reunion with his sister Lenka in Prague in the spring of 1946, they moved on to Paris, hoping that this would prove but a way station en route to Paterson, New Jersey, the home of their uncle, Isadore Minick. America, however, did not want them. France really didn't want them either, but accepted them on sufferance. Their visas were "irregular," to say the least: purloined by a connection from the French embassy, as opposed to being properly processed and officially stamped. They were allowed domicile in Paris only on condition that they report each week to the police. Given their decision to put Poland, the intolerant land of their birth, behind them, the two Mielnickis were, in effect, stateless, rootless, and, as events would prove, without any compensating stability in their sibling relationship.

For, Lenka, at twenty-six, was still a beautiful young woman. Soon she would experience whirlwind romance, marriage, motherhood, French citizenship, and a subsequent career as a beautician. Ultimately, her life had little room for Michel. Their individual Holocaust experiences had shaped them differently

Michel in Paris, 1946.

indeed, compounding, as it were, both their individual strengths and weaknesses. In 1967, Lenka and her husband would immigrate to Israel, where she resides today.

Michel might have wound up in Israel as well. In Breslau in early 1946, he'd volunteered for the Haganah, completed his basic training, and was en route to fight for Israeli independence when he discovered Lenka's existence. Family meant everything to Michel — it always would. At nineteen, experienced in the art of physical survival but innocent in the ways of the world outside the camps, he was about the business of learning most of life's lessons the hard way. He'd already been cheated and robbed of much of the inheritance he had acquired from the sale of his family's Wasilkow properties. Now, his sister's ambitions directed him

June.

away from Palestine to Paris, where he found himself stranded. He was still a hustler, but he had no marketable education or training, and in Paris steady unskilled work was hard to find.

For a while, the Haganah paid part of his rent, in exchange for his provision of small-arms training to new recruits. He ate most often at one of the Jewish community centres. For personal expenses, he was largely dependent on the charity of his American uncles, until they said, "No more." Worse still, most nights he awoke soaked in sweat and screaming at the black-shirted spectres from Birkenau, Dora, and Bergen-Belsen that haunted his dreams.

In such circumstances, one would think that Michel wouldn't have had much of a future, but such was not the case. He was young. He was vital. He was handsome. And the young French women liked him a lot. More important, he was ambitious. He was, after all, the son of Chaim Mielnicki. University might have been out of the question because of the costs involved, but craft training was freely available, and, Paris being Paris, Michel was to find his niche, and his new name, Michel, in the field of fashion design. In due course, and after an arduous apprenticeship, this would turn into the custom design and manufacture of high-fashion creations in ermine, mink, Arctic fox, and sable.

His salvation as a human being, however, came in 1948 when he met his wife-to-be, Frederika (June) Frischer, who was one of three sisters (Dola and Maria were the others) from the ancient Polish city of Cracow, each of whom had survived the Nazi death camps. June married Michel in 1949, and, in due course, provided him with the family he so desperately needed (they were to have two children, Alain and Vivian). More important, perhaps, she was able to give him the understanding, comfort, and strength that only another survivor could provide.

In 1953, the Mielnickis immigrated to Canada, settling in Montreal, where June's two sisters and their husbands had preceded them. It was here that Michel's career blossomed. He would become one of Canada's premiere fur designers, doing stoles, jackets, and full-length coats for the rich and famous, including Princess Beatrix of the Netherlands, for whom he designed a stole of white mink in 1966, on the occasion of her marriage to West German diplomat Claus-Georg von Amsberg. The wives of foreign diplomats, Canadian cabinet ministers, as well as those of the otherwise rich and famous flocked to his salon. Indeed, he designed the full-length brown Alaska seal coat with extra large pockets that Maryon Pearson wore when she journeyed to Russia in 1955 with her husband, Lester B. (Mike) Pearson, Canada's distinguished Secretary of State for External Affairs. Michel's most celebrated commission, however, was to design the mink jacket presented by the Government of Canada to Her Majesty Queen Elizabeth II in 1966 on the occasion of her fortieth birthday. The fashion shows of "Mister Michel," principal fur designer for the Hudson's Bay Company, became transCanada events in the early 1960s, thus acquainting Michel with Vancouver, the city where he and his family have made their lives for the past thirty-one years.

If all Jews are sensitive, as well they might be given their history in the Diaspora, to anything that smacks of anti-Semitism, it would seem reasonable that survivors are even more acutely attuned. Michel had found himself in so many uncomfortable situations in Paris that he stopped identifying himself publicly as a Jew. In fact, it was his experience with French anti-Semitism (as well as some trepidation at the prospect of being drafted into an army that was fighting an unjust and losing war in Indochina) that caused him to reject the opportunity to apply for French citizenship.

Immigration to Canada appeared much the better bet. Unfortunately, Montreal, for all its claims to cosmopolitan sophistication, was the metropolitan centre of a self-defined "captured nation," and its French Canadian Roman Catholic majority often seemed anti-Semitic at its core — as did its British Canadian Protestant minority for that matter. What is more, there were aspects of the collective persona of Montreal's established Jewish community that Michel found exclusionary, and sometimes remarkably unsettling.

The reader, I think, will be interested in the following excerpt from this writer's interviews with Michel about the circumstances surrounding Canada's acceptance of his immigration application:

> *Michel*: When I applied to come to Canada, I talked to a French-Canadian immigration officer. I told him all about me in French, and he kind of got to like me. He said, "Mr. Mielnicki, I see you are of Jewish faith. If I were you, I wouldn't mark that down on your application papers, because it will take a long time, or never. Because the English Canadians don't want to let in Jews. We in Quebec

would gladly accept you because you are French-speaking. But Canada itself doesn't accept Jewish people so easily. This," he said, "is between me and you."

So, I marked the paper "Orthodox," Mielnicki being a Russian name. Russian Orthodox. Within three months, I got the visa. I had to go through the X-rays and this and that. So I had to come to Canada, not as a Jew, but as a Russian Orthodox. But I still don't accuse Canada for that. It's okay.... I detected French Canadian anti-Semitism long before anybody else, because I speak the language. So I knew. I wasn't very happy after I was established. But don't forget, I made a career in Montreal.

In the 1950s, "historical revisionists" denying the Holocaust experience to which people like Michel had been victim and witness began to make an appearance. In 1959, George Lincoln Rockwell's American Nazi party circulated pamphlets in Quebec calling for the "extermination" of all Jews. This was a theme that was picked up by a French Canadian fanatic by the name of Bellefeuille, whose formation of yet another French Canadian neo-fascist party, when exposed by CBC Television, caused the concentration camp survivors in Montreal finally to organize in protest.

At the time, it was estimated that there were approximately 10,000 survivors of Nazi oppression in the Montreal area, the overwhelming majority of whom simply wanted to get on with their displaced lives as best they could, despite the legally sanctioned bigotry that denied them entry to private schools and clubs, various recreational facilities, resorts, golf clubs, and the like. One of the things Michel did to combat the anti-Semitism around him was to become a founding member of the Association of Former Concentration Camp Inmates in October

Michel in the 1964 Montreal survivors' parade.

1960. By 1964, their numbers had grown from an original 50 members to 2,000 men and women parading through the streets, with banners proclaiming:

"HOMAGE TO THE DEAD — WARNING TO THE LIVING."

And at the head of these demonstrations against the renewed forces of Nazi darkness was Michel Mielnicki, *number 98040,* dressed in a reproduction of an Auschwitz prisoner's jacket and cap.

By mid-1966, however, Quebec's Quiet Revolution was developing an increasing nationalist edge, which did not augur well for any of that province's minority populations. To Michel, it was beginning to feel like Poland all over again. And Michel Mielnicki had had enough of that in his life. He'd become a professional success in Montreal, a credit to his adopted country, had invested wisely, but justifiably felt that he should be able to enjoy the fruits

Michel laying wreath commemorating Holocaust victims at Montreal cenotaph.

of his labours without constant worry about the safety of himself and his family. It was time to move on. He told June: "We're selling everything we own, and moving to Vancouver." Over thirty years now have passed. With luck, time will prove Michel's instincts about Quebec wrong.

After a few years in the fashion business in Vancouver, Michel went into semi-retirement in 1970, content to allow his investments to provide a comfortable, although far from lavish, lifestyle for himself and his family. They would travel. The children would go on to college and university. He and June would study art and languages, play tennis and bridge, entertain their friends, and spoil their grandchildren, Rachel, Arry and Eliana. They would help new immigrants to Canada (including Polish gentiles), perform volunteer work, and attend Vancouver's Temple Shalom Reform Synagogue.

Finally, whenever called upon to do so by the Vancouver

Holocaust Education Centre, Michel would talk to students, at levels from elementary school to university, about his experiences in Wasilkow, Bialystok, Pruzany, Birkenau, Monowitz, Dora, Bergen-Belsen, and postwar Poland. *He would always be a witness.*

————

A word or three needs be said about the making of this book. I began interviewing Michel Mielnicki in September 1995. Over the period until December of that year, Michel and I met for some eighty hours. The typed transcription of our interviews exceeded 800 pages (and are available to anyone interested at the Vancouver Holocaust Education Centre). This plus the transcriptions of earlier interviews done with Michel by Phyllis Hamlett, for which she deserves much credit, as well as those by Dr. Robert Krell and Professor William Nicholls, plus transcriptions of various of Michel's talks and lectures, plus such documentation as Michel possessed about his life and career, in addition to secondary source materials on Poland and the Holocaust, provided the basis for the first drafts of this book.

My object was, so far as possible, to make Michel's voice a living part of the text. To make it his book, not mine. My approach in all this was to ferret out as much as I could of the truth of every situation, however horrible this might be. The processs, however, proved particularly stressful for both Michel and me. But most of all for Michel. As he indicates in his Preface, his depression, already clinical, became profound. I can only guess how ghastly this must have been for him. For me, his Holocaust experiences filled my dreams to the point where constant nightmares inter-rupted my sleep, which caused me to begin to worry about my own sanity. An author is often obliged temporarily to suspend his personal being in order to become a clear medium for his subject, but he ought never to lose his own identity in the process. To do so is to fall over the edge. Fortunately, I do not ever have to do another Holocaust story. Michel, on the other hand, will never escape from the one recorded in these pages.

Of course, I too have a number of selected readers and others to thank for their contributions to the improvement of this text. First and foremost, as with every book I either author or edit, there is my wife Joan, who not only transcribes interviews, and proofreads manuscript drafts, but acts as my principal intellectual sounding board. My son Victor did some transcription, and commented intelligently on this manuscript's penultimate draft. My then sixteen-year-old son, Gordon, his friend Devon Saintsbury, and Bronwen Payerle read the manuscript from a gentile North American teenage point of view. I was concerned that Michel's story not be lost on young men and women of the age he was when he entered the death camp at Birkenau. It wasn't.

One of my more mature readers thought Michel very unfair in his assessment of the British, which is probably correct, although irrelevant. Michel is not an historian, he is a witness to history. His opinions and feelings are his own. My job was to see that they were correctly recorded and clearly expressed. On one thing only was there unanimous opinion among our readers, and that was that Michel's was a story worthy of publication, even in a literature as vast as that concerning the Holocaust.

My thanks goes out to my focus-group (manuscript readers): George Brandak, Eric Brown, Renia Perel, John Van Beers, Alexander Wilson, and Darrell Zarn. They will find their editorial suggestions reflected in the text. Finally, I owe a special debt of gratitude to novelist George Payerle for his yeoman service in typing the transcripts of over ninety percent of the tapes, and for his particularly thoughtful comments on a variety of craft problems that plagued this book's early drafts. Editors of my sort, that is those who actually create narrative works from other people's stories, often do themselves require editors.

JOHN MUNRO
VANCOUVER, BRITISH COLUMBIA
10 FEBRUARY 2000

Michel and June at home in Vancouver.

WHERE WERE YOU?

Dear G-d where were you, when we called your name?
Were you just ignoring us, or hiding in shame?
Where were you when nations involved in gigantic clashes
Showed their indifference while our bodies turned into ashes?
Where were you when we were driven mercilessly like beasts,
And the mighty so called super-race was enjoying its feasts?
Did you not hear thousands of our little children's muted cries
When they were starving and killed in front of their parents' eyes?
Oh! why is Providence so cruel to us, and our lives to some only a joke?
Why should millions of innocent, and decent souls go up in smoke?
Oh G-d where were you when we called your name?
Were you just ignoring us or hiding in shame?

GEORGE WERTMAN
MAY 1991

―――――――

JUST A THOUGHT

If our Jewish People for the last two thousand years,
Could have managed by some miracle to preserve our tears,
We could drown in them our enemies, restore our past glory,
And leave to the future generations another biblical story.

GEORGE WERTMAN
FEBRUARY 1996

INDEX